BRAVE O.

Procrastination Unlocked

The Science Behind Getting things Done

First edition

*This book was professionally typeset on Reedsy.
Find out more at reedsy.com*

Contents

1 INTRODUCTION: 1

2 UNDERSTANDING THE ROOT
CAUSES OF PROCRASTINATION   5
The Psychology Behind Procrastination   5
The brain's role in procrastination   11
The procrastination cycle   16

3 THE SCIENCE OF MOTIVATION:
FUELING YOUR DRIVE   21
What motivates you?   21
Dopamine and reward systems   26
Building momentum   31

4 BREAKING DOWN THE BARRIERS
TO ACTION   38
Overcoming perfectionism   38
Managing fear and self-doubt   44
Eliminating distractions   50

5 TIME MANAGEMENT FOR THE
MODERN PROCRASTINATOR   57
Prioritization strategies   57
The power of scheduling   62
Overcoming decision fatigue   68

6 REWIRING YOUR BRAIN FOR PRODUCTIVITY   74
Neuroplasticity and habit formation   74
The role of mindfulness   81

Training your focus 89

7 MASTERING SELF-DISCIPLINE 95

What self-discipline really is 95

Strengthening your willpower 100

Cultivating accountability 105

8 PRACTICAL TOOLS FOR OVER-COMING PROCRASTINATION 112

Leveraging productivity apps and tools 112

The power of checklists 121

Customizing your environment 128

9 MANAGING ENERGY TO MAXI-MIZE PRODUCTIVITY 137

The importance of energy management 137

Nutrition and sleep for focus 144

Exercise and movement 152

10 THE POWER OF REWARDS AND REFLECTION 159

Celebrating small wins 159

Reflecting on progress 166

11 BECOMING A PROACTIVE PERSON 174

Shifting your identity 174

Embracing action-oriented habits 180

Inspiring others to change 186

12 BONUS 193

13 WHAT DISTINGUISH THE BOOK FROM OTHER BOOKS 199

14 CONCLUSION 205

15 QUIZ SECTION 207

16 NOTES 211

1

INTRODUCTION:

Why This Book Will Change the Way You Get Things Done.

Let's be real for a moment. If you're here reading this, procrastination has likely been your loyal—albeit unwanted—companion for too long. You've mastered the art of putting things off, rationalizing delays, and convincing yourself that tomorrow will be the magical day when everything gets done. Spoiler alert: It rarely is. But don't beat yourself up too much. Procrastination isn't a personal failure; it's a universal struggle. The difference between you and the person who seems to "have it all together" isn't superhuman willpower. It's understanding the underlying mechanisms that drive procrastination and learning how to work with, not against, your brain. That's where this book comes in.

Procrastination Unlocked: The Science Behind Getting Things Done isn't just another self-help book filled with clichés like "just do it" or "grind harder." Let's face it: if it were that simple, you wouldn't need this book in the first place. What makes this guide unique is its focus on the science of procrastination. We'll dive deep into the psychological, neurological, and emotional factors that keep you stuck in a cycle of avoidance and frustration. This isn't about quick fixes or fluff; it's about equipping you with proven strategies rooted in research to tackle procrastination at its core.

Here's the truth most books won't tell you: procrastination isn't just about laziness or lack of motivation. It's often tied to fear—fear of failure, fear of imperfection, or even fear of success. Yes, you read that right. Sometimes, the mere thought of achieving what you've set out to do feels overwhelming. Add distractions, unrealistic expectations, and societal pressure to "hustle 24/7," and you've got the perfect storm for procrastination to thrive.

This book is here to cut through the noise. It's here to call you out (with love), make you laugh, and, more importantly, give you the tools you need to turn your procrastination into productivity. Think of it as your personal coach, cheering you on while also holding you accountable. We'll uncover why your brain loves to procrastinate, the tricks it plays to keep you comfortable, and the steps you can take to outsmart it.

But what truly sets this book apart is its blend of practicality and empathy. I'm not here to preach from a pedestal or pretend I've never wrestled with procrastination myself. Trust me, I've been in the trenches. I know what it's like to stare at a to-do list and feel utterly paralyzed. I understand the frustration of knowing what needs to be done but somehow not being able to take that first step. That's why this book is filled with strategies that are actionable, relatable, and adaptable to your unique life and challenges.

And let's not forget the humor. Because let's face it—procrastination is absurd at times. The mental gymnastics we perform to avoid tasks could qualify us for the Olympics. This book will make you laugh at yourself (in the best way) while helping you unravel the habits and beliefs that have held you back.

So, why should you read this book? Because your life is too valuable to be wasted on endless delays and half-finished goals. Because deep down, you know you're capable of so much more. And because you deserve a guide that respects your journey, challenges your excuses, and inspires you to take action.

Why We Procrastinate and Why This Book is Different

Procrastination is a universal challenge. It's not just about putting off tasks; it's a deeper struggle that affects our productivity, our mental well-being, and even our relationships. At its core, procrastination is often driven by emotional triggers like fear, anxiety, or even boredom. We tell ourselves, "I'll do it later," but later turns into days, weeks, or months, and the cycle repeats. This delay creates a heavy burden of guilt and stress, leaving us wondering why we can't just get things done.

Traditional advice like "just try harder" or "be more disciplined" rarely works. These approaches fail to address the root causes of procrastination. That's because procrastination is not just a habit—it's deeply intertwined with how our brains work. It's influenced by the interplay of our emotions, thoughts, and environment. To overcome it, we need more than quick fixes; we need a deeper understanding of why we procrastinate and how we can rewire our behaviors.

This book is different because it's grounded in science and practical strategies. By exploring the neuroscience of decision-making and motivation, we'll uncover why our brains sometimes sabotage our best intentions. This isn't about blaming yourself or shaming you into action. Instead, it's about empowering you with tools and knowledge to overcome procrastination in a sustainable way.

Throughout this journey, you'll find that this book doesn't just tell you what to do—it shows you how to do it. By combining evidence-based techniques with actionable steps, you'll gain a clear roadmap to transform your procrastination habits. This book isn't a one-size-fits-all solution; it's designed to help you tailor these strategies to your own life, making them practical and achievable. Whether you've struggled with procrastination for years or you're just starting to notice its impact, this book will guide you toward becoming the productive, confident, and proactive person you aspire to be.

By the time you finish *Procrastination Unlocked*, you won't just understand why you procrastinate; you'll have a personalized toolkit to overcome it and finally start living up to your potential. Your future self will thank you for taking this step today. No more waiting. It's time to unlock the science behind getting things done and reclaim control over your time, your goals, and your life. Are you ready? Let's dive in.

2

UNDERSTANDING THE ROOT CAUSES OF PROCRASTINATION

The Psychology Behind Procrastination

Procrastination is often misunderstood as laziness or a lack of ambition, but its roots lie much deeper in the human psyche. At its core, procrastination is a complex interplay between our emotions, thoughts, and behaviors. It's not just about avoiding tasks; it's about managing how those tasks make us feel. When faced with a project, responsibility, or decision, our brains weigh the perceived discomfort or difficulty of the task against the temporary relief of postponing it. The result? A short-term escape that ultimately creates more long-term stress.

Emotions play a significant role in procrastination. Tasks that evoke feelings of fear, uncertainty, or inadequacy are often the ones we push aside. For example, if a task seems overwhelming or beyond our abilities, our instinct is to avoid it to shield ourselves from the discomfort of failure or judgment. This avoidance, however, doesn't resolve the underlying issue. Instead, it creates a feedback loop where the longer we delay, the more daunting the task becomes.

On a cognitive level, procrastination is tied to how our brains process rewards. The human brain is wired to prioritize immediate gratification over delayed rewards, a phenomenon that stems from our evolutionary past. This makes it difficult to focus on long-term goals when short-term distractions promise instant pleasure. This tendency, combined with a lack of clear strategies for managing time and effort, can make procrastination feel like an inevitable part of life.

Another significant factor is self-regulation. Procrastination often arises when our ability to self-discipline and manage our impulses is weak. It's not just about willpower; it's about how we structure our environment, set our priorities, and handle competing demands. Without these skills, even the most well-intentioned plans can fall apart.

Understanding the psychology behind procrastination is the first step in overcoming it. It's not about judging ourselves for what we haven't accomplished but about recognizing the patterns and triggers that lead to delay. By addressing these root causes, we can begin to break free from the cycle of procrastination and build habits that support sustained action and progress.

The role of fear, anxiety, and self-doubt.

Fear, anxiety, and self-doubt are some of the most significant emotional forces driving procrastination. They don't just delay action; they create a paralyzing cycle that makes even starting a task feel overwhelming. At their core, these emotions are protective mechanisms. They arise when we perceive a threat—whether it's the possibility of failure, the judgment of others, or the fear of not being good enough. However, rather than helping us, these feelings often backfire, trapping us in a state of inaction.

Fear, in particular, plays a profound role. The fear of failure is one of the most common reasons people procrastinate. When a task or goal feels challenging, fear convinces us that trying and failing would be worse than not trying at all. For example, you might delay submitting a project because you worry it won't meet expectations, or you avoid starting a fitness plan because you're afraid you won't stick to it. This avoidance protects you from immediate discomfort but robs you of the opportunity to grow or succeed.

Anxiety compounds this fear. Tasks that seem daunting often trigger a spiral of "what if" scenarios. What if the presentation is terrible? What if my ideas aren't good enough? This anticipatory anxiety can make the task feel even more overwhelming, creating a mental barrier that seems insurmountable. Ironically, the longer you put off the task, the more the anxiety grows, making it even harder to begin.

Self-doubt is the quiet saboteur that amplifies fear and anxiety. It's the internal voice that tells you, "You're not smart enough," "You're not capable," or "You'll never get this right." This self-criticism erodes your confidence and makes any effort feel futile. When you don't believe in your ability to succeed, it becomes easier to avoid the task altogether.

Together, these emotions create a powerful procrastination loop. Fear and anxiety discourage action, self-doubt undermines confidence, and avoidance reinforces the belief that the task is too difficult. Breaking free from this cycle requires more than just determination—it involves understanding and addressing these emotions head-on. By identifying the fears and doubts that hold you back, reframing your mindset, and building confidence through small, manageable steps, you can begin to dismantle the emotional roadblocks that fuel procrastination.

Instant gratification and the pleasure principle.

Procrastination often thrives on our brain's natural tendency to seek out instant gratification. This is deeply rooted in what psychologists refer to as the pleasure principle—the innate human drive to seek pleasure and avoid pain. When we encounter tasks that seem tedious, challenging, or even slightly uncomfortable, our brain starts looking for an escape. That escape often comes in the form of activities that offer immediate rewards, like scrolling through social media, watching TV, or indulging in other distractions.

The allure of instant gratification is powerful because it provides an immediate dopamine boost. Dopamine, the brain's "feel-good" chemical, is released when we do something enjoyable, reinforcing the behavior and encouraging us to repeat it. For example, answering a text message or checking notifications feels rewarding in the moment, even though it pulls us away from more important tasks. This creates a cycle where short-term pleasure takes precedence over long-term goals, making it harder to stay focused on meaningful work.

The problem with instant gratification is that its rewards are fleeting. While it may feel good to put off a difficult task in favor of something enjoyable, the satisfaction is temporary. The task you've avoided doesn't disappear; it lingers in the background, growing larger and more intimidating over time. This leads to a buildup of stress and guilt, which can then make the original task feel even more overwhelming. Paradoxically, the pursuit of short-term relief often results in long-term discomfort.

Another factor at play is the way our brains weigh the value of immediate rewards against delayed rewards. Psychologists call this "temporal discounting." A task with a distant payoff, like studying for an exam or working on a long-term project, feels less motivating compared to something that offers instant enjoyment. Even when we logically know that completing the task will lead to greater benefits in the future, the immediate allure of gratification can override our intentions.

Breaking free from the grip of instant gratification requires conscious effort. It involves recognizing how the pleasure principle influences your decisions and learning to delay short-term rewards in favor of long-term success. By building awareness of these tendencies and developing strategies to manage them—such as setting boundaries for distractions or breaking tasks into smaller, more manageable steps— you can train your brain to prioritize what truly matters. Over time, the satisfaction of accomplishing meaningful goals becomes its own reward, outweighing the fleeting pleasure of procrastination.

How low self-discipline contributes to delay.

Self-discipline is often seen as the cornerstone of productivity and success, but when it is lacking, procrastination becomes an almost inevitable consequence. Low self-discipline undermines our ability to prioritize long-term goals over short-term impulses, leaving us vulnerable to distractions, temptations, and the urge to avoid challenging tasks. It's not that people with low self-discipline don't want to succeed; rather, they struggle to bridge the gap between their intentions and their actions.

One of the main ways low self-discipline contributes to procrastination is by weakening our ability to resist immediate gratification. Imagine planning to spend the evening working on an important project, but instead, you find yourself binge-watching a series or scrolling through social media. The intention to work is there, but without the self-discipline to resist distractions, the allure of instant pleasure easily takes over. This lack of control reinforces procrastination, making it harder to break the cycle.

Another challenge is the difficulty of initiating tasks, especially those that require sustained effort or feel overwhelming. People with low self-discipline often struggle to push past the initial discomfort of starting a task. This hesitation can be fueled by perfectionism, fear of failure, or simply a lack of motivation. Without the mental resilience to overcome these barriers, even small tasks can feel insurmountable, leading to delays that compound over time.

Additionally, low self-discipline often goes hand-in-hand with poor habits and a lack of structure. Without clear routines, systems, or goals, it becomes easier to drift through the day without making meaningful progress. For example, not setting specific times for work, neglecting to create to-do lists, or failing to prioritize tasks can leave you feeling disorganized and unproductive. This lack of structure not only makes procrastination more likely but also erodes confidence, creating a sense of helplessness that further undermines self-discipline.

The good news is that self-discipline is not a fixed trait; it's a skill that can be developed with practice. By starting small—such as committing to five minutes of focused work or setting achievable daily goals—you can begin to build the habits and mental resilience needed to overcome procrastination. Over time, these small wins add up, strengthening your ability to stay on track and reducing the likelihood of delays. The key is to recognize that self-discipline isn't about being perfect; it's about consistently making choices that align with your long-term goals, even when it feels difficult in the moment.

The brain's role in procrastination

Procrastination is not simply a matter of poor time management or lack of willpower; it is deeply influenced by the complex workings of the brain. At its core, procrastination reflects a struggle between different regions of the brain that have competing priorities. This internal conflict shapes how we make decisions, regulate emotions, and approach tasks. Understanding this dynamic can shed light on why procrastination feels so automatic and why it can be so difficult to overcome.

The brain is constantly balancing immediate desires with

long-term goals, but these two drives often come into conflict. When faced with a task, your brain evaluates the potential rewards and discomforts associated with it. Tasks that feel challenging, boring, or overwhelming tend to activate the brain's emotional centers, which seek to minimize stress and discomfort. This instinctive response pushes you toward activities that provide instant relief or pleasure, even if they have no real value in the long run.

One of the brain's key challenges in avoiding procrastination lies in how it processes rewards. Activities that offer immediate gratification—like scrolling through social media or watching TV—trigger a release of dopamine, the chemical associated with pleasure and reward. This dopamine rush reinforces the behavior, making it even more likely that you'll turn to these distractions the next time you feel stressed or unmotivated. In contrast, tasks with delayed rewards, such as completing a long-term project or studying for an exam, do not provide the same instant dopamine boost. As a result, the brain perceives them as less appealing, even when logic tells you they are important.

Another layer of complexity comes from how the brain handles decisions and emotions. Procrastination often arises from a deep emotional response to a task, such as fear of failure or feelings of inadequacy. These emotions can hijack your ability to think clearly and rationally about the task at hand, making it harder to get started. Over time, avoiding the task becomes a way to temporarily escape these negative emotions, creating a cycle of procrastination that reinforces itself.

The brain's role in procrastination is not all negative, however. By understanding the mechanisms at play, it becomes possible to outsmart your instincts and create habits that encourage productivity. Small adjustments—like breaking tasks into manageable steps, setting clear goals, or creating external accountability—can help you work with your brain rather than against it. Recognizing that procrastination is rooted in biology, not just behavior, is the first step toward breaking free from its grip.

The prefrontal cortex vs. the limbic system.

Procrastination is not just a behavioral habit; it's deeply influenced by the way our brain operates. Two key players in this process are the prefrontal cortex and the limbic system, each with distinct roles. The prefrontal cortex, located at the front of the brain, is responsible for rational thinking, planning, and decision-making. It helps us weigh options, consider long-term consequences, and exercise self-control. When functioning effectively, the prefrontal cortex enables us to stay focused on goals and resist distractions.

On the other hand, the limbic system, an older and more primitive part of the brain, is responsible for our emotional responses and instincts. It drives behaviors that seek pleasure and avoid discomfort, often operating on autopilot. The limbic system is where procrastination begins, as it instinctively gravitates toward activities that feel immediately rewarding or comforting. In contrast, the prefrontal cortex struggles to override these impulses when a task feels difficult, boring, or overwhelming.

This tug-of-war between the prefrontal cortex and the limbic system explains why procrastination is so challenging to overcome. The limbic system demands instant gratification, while the prefrontal cortex tries to enforce discipline and focus. However, when the prefrontal cortex is tired, distracted, or overwhelmed, it often loses the battle, allowing the limbic system to dominate. Understanding this dynamic is key to developing strategies that strengthen the prefrontal cortex's ability to regulate behavior and keep procrastination in check.

Why we prioritize short-term rewards.

The brain is naturally wired to prioritize immediate rewards over long-term benefits, a tendency rooted in evolutionary biology. In the past, prioritizing short-term needs, such as food and safety, was essential for survival. While this trait served our ancestors well, it now poses challenges in modern life, where long-term goals often take precedence over immediate needs.

This preference for short-term rewards is driven by the brain's reward system, particularly the release of dopamine. When we engage in activities like watching a funny video or snacking on a treat, dopamine floods the brain, creating a sense of pleasure. This instant gratification feels good in the moment and reinforces the behavior, making us more likely to repeat it. Tasks with delayed rewards, such as completing a project or studying for an exam, don't provide the same immediate dopamine boost, making them less appealing.

As a result, even when we know a task is important, the brain struggles to prioritize it over more gratifying distractions. This is why checking notifications or streaming a favorite show often feels more tempting than tackling responsibilities. Recognizing this tendency can help us implement strategies to delay gratification and focus on long-term rewards. By intentionally shifting how we frame and approach tasks, we can train our brain to find satisfaction in progress and completion, rather than fleeting pleasures.

The science of motivation and decision-making.

Motivation and decision-making are two key processes that influence procrastination, and both are deeply rooted in brain function. Motivation is the drive to take action, and it often depends on how the brain perceives the value of a task. If a task feels too difficult, boring, or overwhelming, the brain devalues it, making it harder to muster the energy to begin. Conversely, when a task is seen as rewarding or achievable, motivation increases, and action becomes more likely.

Decision-making, meanwhile, involves weighing the costs and benefits of taking action. This process relies heavily on the prefrontal cortex, which assesses the consequences of our choices and helps us prioritize. However, when faced with a choice between an unpleasant task and an enjoyable distraction, the brain often leans toward the option that feels easier or more rewarding in the moment. This bias toward immediate comfort is a major factor in procrastination.

The science of motivation also reveals that breaking tasks into smaller, manageable steps can significantly improve our ability to act. Each small accomplishment triggers a dopamine release, reinforcing positive behavior and building momentum. Similarly, setting clear goals and creating a sense of urgency can help the brain stay focused on what matters most. By understanding how motivation and decision-making work, we can create environments and habits that support consistent action and reduce the likelihood of delay.

The procrastination cycle

The procrastination cycle is a self-reinforcing loop that keeps people stuck in patterns of delay and avoidance, often despite their best intentions. It begins with a task that feels daunting, unpleasant, or emotionally charged. This initial discomfort triggers avoidance behaviors, as the brain seeks to escape the negative emotions associated with the task. In the short term, avoiding the task provides relief—a momentary reprieve that feels comforting and even justified. However, this relief is fleeting and ultimately adds to the problem.

As time passes, the task doesn't go away. Instead, it lingers in the back of your mind, creating a growing sense of unease. Deadlines creep closer, and the pressure to complete the task mounts. This intensifies feelings of stress and guilt, which in turn make the task feel even more overwhelming. With these heightened emotions, the brain defaults to its natural response: seeking comfort and avoiding discomfort. The cycle repeats itself, and the task remains undone, often until the very last minute or beyond.

This loop is not merely behavioral; it's deeply tied to emotional and cognitive processes. Procrastination often feeds on internal doubts and fears, such as a fear of failure or perfectionism. These feelings can magnify the perceived difficulty of a task, creating an inflated barrier to starting. Each time you avoid the task, you reinforce the belief that it's too hard or that you're incapable of handling it, which makes it even harder to begin the next time.

Breaking free from the procrastination cycle requires disrupting this loop at its various stages. Awareness is the first step: recognizing when the cycle is starting and understanding the emotions and thoughts driving the behavior. From there, small, deliberate actions can help shift the momentum, replacing avoidance with progress. The cycle doesn't have to define your relationship with tasks; it's possible to interrupt it and create a new pattern that prioritizes action and accomplishment. By acknowledging the cycle and its impact, you can take meaningful steps toward reclaiming control and achieving your goals.

Identifying your triggers.

Procrastination often starts with triggers—specific situations, emotions, or thoughts that prompt us to delay action. These triggers can be subtle or obvious, but they consistently lead to the same outcome: avoidance. For some, the trigger might be the sight of a daunting task, like a blank document waiting to be filled. For others, it might be an overwhelming sense of perfectionism or fear of failure that makes even starting seem impossible. Triggers often tap into deeper emotional responses, such as anxiety, frustration, or a lack of confidence, which push us toward distraction as a form of temporary relief.

Recognizing your triggers is a crucial step in breaking the procrastination cycle. Without awareness, these moments of avoidance often feel automatic, leaving little room for conscious decision-making. By identifying the specific situations or feelings that make you procrastinate, you can begin to address the underlying issues and develop strategies to counteract them. For example, if you find yourself avoiding tasks that seem too complex, breaking them into smaller, actionable steps can make them feel less overwhelming. Similarly, if emotional triggers like self-doubt are at play, practicing self-compassion and focusing on progress rather than perfection can help shift your mindset.

How small delays snowball into bigger issues.

Procrastination often begins with a small delay—putting off a task for an hour, a day, or even a week. In the moment, this delay can feel harmless, even justifiable. After all, what's the harm in giving yourself a little more time to tackle something difficult or unpleasant? However, these small delays rarely remain isolated incidents. Instead, they tend to snowball, growing into larger and more complex problems over time.

When you delay a task, it doesn't simply disappear. It lingers in the back of your mind, creating a sense of unfinished business that can lead to stress and guilt. As the deadline looms closer, the pressure to complete the task increases, but so does the temptation to avoid it. This creates a feedback loop: the more stressed you feel about the task, the harder it becomes to start, leading to further delays. What began as a small postponement can quickly escalate into a full-blown crisis, where the task feels insurmountable and time is running out.

The snowball effect of procrastination can also have a ripple impact on other areas of your life. For instance, delaying one task might force you to rush through others, lowering the quality of your work and creating additional stress. It can also erode your confidence, as repeated delays reinforce the belief that you're incapable of following through. Over time, this pattern can damage your sense of self-efficacy, making it harder to break free from the cycle of procrastination.

Breaking this pattern requires acknowledging the long-term consequences of small delays. While it's natural to want to avoid discomfort in the moment, recognizing how these choices compound over time can motivate you to take action sooner rather than later. Even a small step toward completing a task can interrupt the snowball effect, restoring a sense of control and momentum.

Recognizing unhelpful habits.

Procrastination is often sustained by a set of unhelpful habits that have become deeply ingrained over time. These habits can include mindlessly scrolling through social media, endlessly reorganizing your workspace, or convincing yourself that you work better under pressure. While these behaviors might provide temporary relief or distraction, they ultimately keep you stuck in a cycle of avoidance. Recognizing these habits is essential for breaking free from procrastination and replacing them with more constructive behaviors.

Unhelpful habits are often born out of a desire to avoid discomfort. For example, instead of diving into a challenging task, you might opt to clean your desk, telling yourself that you're preparing to be more productive. While this might feel productive in the moment, it's often a form of procrastination in disguise. Similarly, habits like checking your phone "just for a minute" can quickly spiral into hours of lost time, leaving you even further behind. These behaviors are reinforced by the brain's reward system, which values the immediate gratification they provide, even at the expense of long-term progress.

Recognizing these patterns requires honest self-reflection. It's important to ask yourself whether your actions are genuinely moving you closer to your goals or simply serving as a distraction. Once you've identified your unhelpful habits, you can begin to replace them with more intentional choices. This might involve setting boundaries for distractions, such as putting your phone in another room, or establishing clear routines that prioritize your most important tasks. By breaking the hold of these habits, you can create an environment that supports productivity rather than undermines it.

Ultimately, the key to breaking the procrastination cycle lies in awareness and intentionality. By understanding your triggers, acknowledging the snowball effect of delays, and addressing unhelpful habits, you can begin to reclaim your time and energy, setting yourself up for lasting success.

3

THE SCIENCE OF MOTIVATION: FUELING YOUR DRIVE

What motivates you?

Motivation is the driving force behind every action we take, from the smallest tasks to our loftiest ambitions. It's what gets us out of bed in the morning and keeps us moving forward, even in the face of challenges. Yet, understanding what truly motivates us can often feel elusive. We may find ourselves energized and productive one day, only to struggle with inertia the next, wondering why the spark has faded. This fluctuation in motivation is not random; it is deeply tied to how we perceive the tasks before us, the rewards we associate with them, and the alignment of those tasks with our personal values and desires.

At its core, motivation is about purpose. When you understand why you are doing something, it becomes easier to push through difficulties and distractions. Purpose doesn't have to be grand or life-changing; even small, meaningful reasons can provide the momentum needed to act. For example, you might complete a task because it supports a larger goal, helps someone you care about, or simply brings a sense of satisfaction. On the other hand, when purpose is absent, tasks often feel like burdens. They lack the emotional or intellectual connection needed to spark action, leaving you disengaged and prone to delay.

Motivation is also influenced by how we frame success and progress. Some people are motivated by achieving specific goals, while others thrive on the journey itself, finding joy in the process rather than just the outcome. Reflecting on what motivates you most—whether it's the sense of accomplishment at the finish line or the growth you experience along the way—can help you structure your approach to tasks in a way that feels natural and rewarding.

Another important aspect of motivation is how it responds to internal and external factors. Internal motivation, driven by your own values and interests, often creates a deeper and more lasting sense of fulfillment. External motivation, such as rewards or recognition, can be a powerful catalyst but may not sustain long-term effort if it's not paired with a genuine personal connection to the work. Balancing these forces is key to maintaining momentum.

Ultimately, understanding what motivates you requires introspection and experimentation. It involves asking yourself what you care about, what energizes you, and what makes you feel accomplished. It's not a one-size-fits-all solution but a personal journey that evolves over time. By exploring your motivations and aligning them with your goals, you can create a framework for action that feels both authentic and sustainable.

Intrinsic vs. extrinsic motivation.

Motivation can be broadly categorized into two types: intrinsic and extrinsic. Intrinsic motivation arises from within, fueled by an internal desire to engage in an activity because it is personally rewarding or aligns with your values and interests. It's the kind of drive that pushes someone to learn a new skill simply for the joy of mastering it or to complete a challenging project because of the deep satisfaction it brings. This form of motivation is often more sustainable because it connects directly to what feels meaningful and fulfilling on a personal level.

Extrinsic motivation, on the other hand, is driven by external rewards or pressures. It might stem from a desire to earn recognition, financial rewards, or approval from others, or to avoid negative consequences such as criticism or penalties. While extrinsic motivation can be effective in the short term, it often lacks the depth and endurance of intrinsic motivation. Tasks driven solely by external forces may feel hollow or burdensome, leading to a reliance on external validation to maintain momentum.

The balance between these two forms of motivation is key. While intrinsic motivation tends to foster deeper engagement and enjoyment, extrinsic factors can provide an initial push, especially for tasks that don't immediately seem meaningful or enjoyable. The challenge lies in finding ways to align your external obligations with your internal values, creating a synergy that keeps you motivated even when external rewards are absent. Understanding what motivates you at both levels can help you harness the right kind of energy to stay productive and fulfilled.

Finding personal meaning in tasks.

One of the most powerful ways to combat procrastination is by uncovering the personal meaning behind the tasks you undertake. When a task feels disconnected from your values or goals, it's easy to put it off indefinitely. Conversely, when you can see how a task contributes to something important to you—whether it's personal growth, career advancement, or helping others—it becomes easier to muster the energy and focus to complete it.

Finding meaning doesn't always happen naturally; it often requires intentional reflection. For example, you might initially view an assignment as just another obligation. But by digging deeper, you may realize that completing it could help you develop a skill you've always wanted to improve or open doors to new opportunities. Even mundane tasks, like organizing your workspace or responding to emails, can take on new significance when viewed through the lens of how they support your broader goals.

Reframing tasks in this way doesn't make them easier, but it does make them feel more worthwhile. When you connect your actions to a greater purpose, you tap into a sense of fulfillment that transcends the immediate discomfort or tedium of the task. This perspective shift can transform your relationship with productivity, helping you approach even the most challenging tasks with a renewed sense of purpose and commitment.

The role of autonomy in productivity.

Autonomy, or the ability to make choices and have control over your actions, plays a significant role in sustaining motivation and productivity. When you feel empowered to make decisions about how, when, and where you complete a task, it fosters a sense of ownership and accountability. This sense of control is often linked to intrinsic motivation, as it allows you to align your actions with your personal preferences and values.

Conversely, when tasks feel imposed or overly controlled by external forces, motivation tends to wane. A lack of autonomy can create feelings of resentment or apathy, making it harder to engage with the work at hand. This is why micromanagement or rigid structures often lead to diminished productivity and increased procrastination. Without the freedom to approach tasks in a way that feels natural or effective to you, even small obstacles can feel insurmountable.

To enhance autonomy, it's important to focus on areas where you can exercise choice, even within externally defined constraints. This might mean prioritizing tasks based on your energy levels, customizing your workflow to suit your strengths, or setting your own milestones within a larger project. By cultivating a sense of agency, you can create an environment that supports sustained effort and engagement, ultimately making it easier to overcome procrastination and achieve your goals. Autonomy is not just about freedom; it's about fostering a mindset where you feel empowered to take action and make progress on your own terms.

Dopamine and reward systems

Dopamine is one of the brain's most influential neurotransmitters, playing a central role in shaping behavior and motivation. Often referred to as the brain's "feel-good" chemical, it is intricately tied to the reward system, driving us to seek out and repeat behaviors that are perceived as pleasurable or beneficial. However, dopamine is not just about experiencing joy; it is equally, if not more, about the anticipation of a reward. This anticipation creates a surge of energy and focus, urging us to act in ways that align with achieving the desired outcome.

The reward system itself is a sophisticated network in the brain, designed to reinforce behaviors that ensure survival, growth, and personal satisfaction. When you accomplish something, whether it's finishing a task, solving a problem, or achieving a goal, your brain rewards you with a burst of dopamine, creating a sense of accomplishment. Over time, this process builds patterns, where certain actions become associated with the release of dopamine, encouraging you to repeat those actions. This is how habits form, for better or worse.

Yet, this same system that drives productivity and goal-oriented behavior can also become a stumbling block when it comes to procrastination. The brain is naturally drawn to activities that offer immediate gratification—those that release dopamine quickly and effortlessly. This is why scrolling through social media, playing games, or indulging in comfort food often feels more appealing than tackling a challenging task. These activities provide quick dopamine hits without requiring significant effort, creating a cycle of short-term pleasure that distracts from long-term goals.

Understanding dopamine and the reward system is crucial for overcoming procrastination. By recognizing how your brain responds to different stimuli and how it prioritizes rewards, you can begin to shift its focus. Rather than relying on fleeting, low-effort dopamine triggers, you can rewire your reward system to find joy and satisfaction in meaningful progress and achievements. This process takes time and intention but ultimately transforms how you approach work, goals, and productivity.

How dopamine drives behavior.

Dopamine is often considered the brain's motivational engine, guiding us toward actions and decisions that promise reward or satisfaction. It's a neurotransmitter with a complex role, not only delivering feelings of pleasure but also encouraging us to seek out and repeat behaviors that seem beneficial or enjoyable. This makes dopamine integral to shaping habits, setting goals, and driving both short-term and long-term behavior.

What makes dopamine so powerful is its role in anticipation. The release of dopamine isn't limited to the moment of achieving a reward; much of its impact lies in the buildup of excitement or expectation leading up to it. When you think about an outcome you desire—whether it's completing a project, winning a game, or indulging in a treat—dopamine surges, creating a sense of urgency and focus that propels you toward the goal. This anticipation keeps you engaged, as your brain essentially signals that the effort is worth it.

However, the same mechanisms that drive positive behavior can also reinforce procrastination. Dopamine is naturally tied to immediate gratification because quick, easily attainable rewards trigger the brain's pleasure centers more effectively than distant or abstract goals. This is why tasks that feel overwhelming or offer no immediate payoff often fail to stimulate dopamine release. Instead, the brain seeks alternatives—like checking your phone or watching TV—that provide faster dopamine hits with minimal effort. Over time, this creates a cycle where unproductive habits are reinforced while meaningful work is postponed.

The way dopamine drives behavior underscores the importance of designing your environment and habits to align with your goals. By understanding how dopamine responds to rewards, you can harness its power to build motivation. Whether it's by breaking large tasks into smaller, more manageable pieces or incorporating immediate, tangible rewards into your routine, you can train your brain to associate productivity with satisfaction. This not only improves your ability to complete tasks but also reshapes how you perceive effort and reward, making meaningful progress feel as rewarding as instant gratification.

Hacking your brain's reward system.

The brain's reward system is a powerful tool, designed to motivate action and reinforce behavior through the release of dopamine. However, this system, while essential for survival and achievement, doesn't inherently prioritize long-term goals or complex tasks. It is naturally wired to seek immediate gratification, which can lead to procrastination when long-term rewards feel distant or abstract. The concept of "hacking" this system involves aligning its natural tendencies with your objectives, creating an environment where productive behavior feels just as rewarding as more effortless distractions.

One effective way to hack the reward system is to break down tasks into smaller, achievable steps. Large, overwhelming goals often fail to trigger dopamine because the brain perceives them as too far away to be satisfying. In contrast, smaller milestones provide a sense of immediate progress, releasing dopamine with each accomplishment. For example, instead of focusing on finishing an entire project, you might set a goal to complete one section or work for a specific amount of time. Each completed step becomes a micro-reward, keeping your brain engaged and motivated to continue.

Another strategy is to introduce intentional rewards for completing tasks. These can be as simple as enjoying a break, indulging in a favorite snack, or taking a few moments to celebrate your progress. Pairing these rewards with productive activities retrains your brain to associate effort with positive outcomes, effectively rewiring the reward system to prioritize work over avoidance. Over time, the anticipation of these rewards can help override the pull of less productive dopamine triggers, like scrolling through social media or watching videos.

Additionally, you can use curiosity and novelty to engage your brain's reward system. Dopamine is not just released by achieving goals but also by exploring new ideas, learning something interesting, or approaching a task from a fresh perspective. When you infuse variety or creativity into your work, the process itself becomes rewarding, reducing the need to rely solely on external motivators.

Hacking your brain's reward system is about working

with its natural wiring instead of fighting against it. By understanding how dopamine influences your actions, you can create an approach to work and productivity that feels satisfying and sustainable. Over time, this helps to build habits that align your short-term impulses with your long-term ambitions, making progress not only achievable but genuinely enjoyable.

Creating micro-rewards for progress.

Micro-rewards are small, intentional incentives that you give yourself for making progress on a task, no matter how minor that progress might seem. They work by leveraging your brain's reward system to reinforce positive behavior, making even the smallest achievements feel satisfying and worthwhile. The beauty of micro-rewards lies in their simplicity—they don't need to be elaborate or extravagant to be effective. Instead, they focus on creating a consistent stream of positive reinforcement that keeps you motivated and engaged.

When you're working on a large or complex task, it's easy to feel overwhelmed by the enormity of what needs to be done. This sense of overwhelm often leads to procrastination because the brain struggles to see a clear path to the reward at the end. Micro-rewards counteract this by breaking the task into smaller, more manageable parts, with each step offering its own immediate payoff. For example, completing 30 minutes of focused work might earn you a short walk, a cup of coffee, or a few minutes to check your favorite app. These small but tangible rewards trigger the release of dopamine, creating a sense of accomplishment and motivating you to continue.

The effectiveness of micro-rewards also lies in their ability to shift your perception of effort. Tasks that once felt tedious or daunting can become more engaging when paired with a reward system. For instance, if you struggle to start a project, you might promise yourself a small treat after writing the first paragraph or completing the first 10 minutes of work. This approach turns the process of working into a series of achievable milestones, each one providing a moment of satisfaction that encourages further progress.

Creating micro-rewards also helps to build momentum. As you accumulate small victories, your confidence and motivation grow, making it easier to tackle more challenging aspects of the task. Over time, the association between effort and reward strengthens, helping to rewire your brain to see productivity as inherently rewarding. By integrating micro-rewards into your routine, you can transform procrastination into progress, one small step—and one dopamine boost—at a time.

Building momentum

Momentum is one of the most powerful forces in overcoming procrastination and sustaining productivity. It's not just about accomplishing tasks; it's about creating a continuous flow of energy and action that carries you forward. When you think of momentum in the context of personal effort, it's the process of turning small, deliberate actions into a steady rhythm that leads to meaningful progress. It's not born out of grand gestures or intense bursts of effort but from consistent, intentional steps that build upon each other over time.

The essence of momentum lies in its compounding nature. Each completed action, no matter how minor, fuels the next. It's as though every step forward builds confidence, reinforces motivation, and reduces the psychological weight of what lies ahead. This cumulative effect makes large or complex goals feel less intimidating because they are approached incrementally rather than all at once. Momentum shifts the focus from the enormity of the destination to the satisfaction of continual movement, transforming what once felt overwhelming into something manageable and even enjoyable.

What makes momentum so effective is its ability to override inertia. In the beginning, taking the first step often feels like the hardest part, much like pushing a heavy object at rest. Once that initial effort is made, however, it becomes easier to keep going. The key is to trust the process of beginning, even when the outcome feels distant or uncertain. By simply starting, you unlock the potential for movement, and that movement gradually builds into something powerful and unstoppable.

Momentum also creates a sense of rhythm and routine that becomes self-reinforcing. Over time, the act of progressing toward a goal begins to feel natural and habitual, reducing the effort required to sustain it. This is why momentum is such a valuable tool—it not only helps you get started but also keeps you going, allowing you to achieve more than you initially thought possible. It's a reminder that productivity is not about perfection or intensity but about consistent forward motion, no matter how small the steps may seem.

The science of starting small.

Starting small is a powerful psychological and neurological strategy that makes tackling large, overwhelming tasks feel more achievable. When faced with a daunting goal or project, the brain often reacts with resistance due to the perceived difficulty or scale of the task. This resistance stems from the activation of stress-related areas of the brain, such as the amygdala, which triggers feelings of fear or anxiety. In response, the brain can easily fall into a state of avoidance or procrastination, making it difficult to get started.

However, starting small minimizes this resistance by creating an easily attainable entry point. When you break a large task into a smaller, more manageable action, it reduces the complexity and removes much of the psychological pressure. This process works by activating the brain's reward system in a subtle yet effective way. Completing small, simple actions generates a sense of accomplishment and releases dopamine, the brain's "feel-good" neurotransmitter. This release not only makes you feel good about completing a task, but it also strengthens your motivation to continue.

Additionally, starting small taps into the principle of cognitive ease. The brain naturally gravitates toward tasks that feel easy or low-effort, and when you focus on a small, easy-to-complete action, it lowers the cognitive load. The less effort your brain perceives is required, the more likely you are to begin and continue working. This is why strategies like setting a timer for just five minutes or committing to writing one paragraph rather than an entire report are so effective—they reduce the mental burden, making the task feel less intimidating.

The science also supports that once you start, momentum takes over. The initial small step activates the brain's motor system, creating a neural pathway that builds on itself with each successive action. Over time, these small steps accumulate, gradually transforming into a habit and creating a snowball effect of productivity. Starting small is not just a technique for overcoming procrastination; it's a fundamental principle that makes large tasks feel less daunting, engages the brain's reward system, and sets the stage for sustained effort and success.

Why consistency beats intensity.

The principle of consistency over intensity is grounded in both neuroscience and behavioral psychology, offering a more sustainable and effective approach to productivity and personal growth. While intense bursts of effort can be motivating in the short term, they often lead to burnout or stagnation if not followed by periods of rest or recovery. The brain, in particular, is not designed for prolonged high-intensity efforts; it thrives on regularity and repetition, where small, consistent actions accumulate over time to produce significant results.

From a neurological perspective, consistency helps build and strengthen neural pathways. Repeated actions create stronger connections in the brain, making it easier to perform tasks with less cognitive effort over time. This is the basis for habit formation: as you consistently engage in a behavior, the brain's circuitry adapts, making the action more automatic. In contrast, intense bursts of effort don't have the same long-term impact on neural plasticity, often requiring a conscious effort to re-engage each time, which can be mentally taxing.

Consistency also fosters a sense of progress and accomplishment, which is key to maintaining motivation. When you focus on small, consistent steps, you are able to see regular progress, even if it's slow. This ongoing sense of achievement reinforces your brain's reward system, creating positive feedback loops that encourage continued effort. Intensity, on the other hand, often leads to periods of exhaustion or plateauing, which can be discouraging and cause you to lose momentum.

Another benefit of consistency is that it reduces the stress and cognitive load associated with trying to complete large tasks all at once. By breaking goals into manageable, repeatable actions, you can gradually chip away at them without feeling overwhelmed. This steady progress allows for a more balanced approach, where the task doesn't feel like a monumental challenge that requires an all-or-nothing effort. Instead, consistency emphasizes the power of showing up regularly, even if the effort is modest. Over time, these repeated efforts build a momentum that intensity alone cannot sustain, making consistent action not only more effective but also more emotionally rewarding.

Ultimately, consistency allows for long-term growth and mastery. Intensity may spark initial motivation, but it is consistency that allows you to refine your skills, build resilience, and achieve lasting results. When you commit to consistent effort, you're setting yourself up for success in a way that's sustainable, emotionally manageable, and aligned with how the brain best functions for progress.

Developing a habit loop.

A habit loop is a powerful concept rooted in behavioral science that explains how habits are formed and reinforced over time. It consists of three primary components: the cue, the routine, and the reward. This loop is at the core of how behaviors become automatic and ingrained in daily life, shaping the way we approach tasks and challenges. The key to developing a productive habit loop is to intentionally design and reinforce each of these components to promote consistency and positive outcomes.

The first component of a habit loop is the **cue**, which triggers the behavior. This could be an external event, a time of day, or an internal feeling. For example, you might feel a sense of stress (the cue), which leads you to engage in a habitual coping mechanism, like procrastination or avoidance. Alternatively, you could set a specific time each day to work on a task, such as starting your writing session every morning at 9 AM. Identifying and establishing a clear cue is crucial because it signals to your brain that it's time to enter into the habitual behavior, making it easier to get started.

The second component is the **routine** itself—the behavior or action that follows the cue. In the context of building positive habits, this is the action you want to repeat consistently, like reading for 10 minutes, working for 30 minutes, or practicing a new skill. The more frequently you repeat this routine after the cue, the more automatic it becomes. The key to success here is repetition. The more you engage in the routine, the stronger the neural connections become, and over time, this action feels less like an effort and more like an ingrained part of your daily routine.

The third and final component is the **reward**, which reinforces the behavior and encourages the brain to repeat it. The reward serves as positive reinforcement, telling your brain that the action was worthwhile. This could be something tangible, like a treat or a break, or it could be an internal feeling of satisfaction or accomplishment. The reward doesn't have to be grand; even small rewards like a few minutes of relaxation, a favorite snack, or a sense of completion after a task can be highly effective. The more immediate and satisfying the reward, the more likely it is that the habit loop will stick.

To develop a strong habit loop, it's essential to make sure that the cue, routine, and reward are aligned and consistent. For example, if your goal is to develop a habit of exercising every morning, your cue might be waking up, your routine would be doing a 10-minute stretch or workout, and your reward could be enjoying a healthy smoothie afterward. By repeating this loop, the behavior becomes ingrained, and over time, the routine becomes automatic, requiring less effort and willpower to continue.

One of the most powerful aspects of a habit loop is its ability to reduce decision fatigue. Instead of debating whether or not to complete a task, the habit loop turns it into a predictable, almost effortless sequence. Developing a habit loop also reduces the mental friction associated with starting new behaviors because once the cue is triggered, the routine follows naturally. The key to success is consistency—if you persist in repeating the loop, the behavior will eventually become second nature, and the habit will be sustained without conscious thought.

4

BREAKING DOWN THE BARRIERS TO ACTION

Overcoming perfectionism

Perfectionism can be both a driving force and a significant barrier to productivity. While high standards can push us to achieve great things, they can also lead to feelings of anxiety, stress, and ultimately, procrastination. This is because the pursuit of perfection often leads to a state of paralysis, where the fear of not meeting an impossible standard prevents action. The key to overcoming this lies in adjusting one's mindset and adopting more practical strategies that focus on progress rather than perfection.

How perfectionism leads to paralysis.

Perfectionism, at its core, is the belief that anything less than flawless is unacceptable. This mindset often creates immense pressure, as it sets an impossibly high standard for success. The problem with perfectionism is that it doesn't allow room for mistakes, adjustments, or learning from failure—all essential components of growth and progress. Instead of motivating individuals to take action, the overwhelming desire to do something perfectly can have the opposite effect: it paralyzes them.

When someone is driven by perfectionism, they may feel that any misstep or imperfection will result in failure or judgment. This fear of not meeting their own or others' high expectations often leads to avoidance. Instead of starting or completing a task, they become caught in an endless cycle of planning, revising, and doubting. The more they focus on the need for perfection, the more they become overwhelmed by the task at hand. This sense of overwhelm leads to procrastination— delaying the task in hopes of achieving a flawless result, which, ironically, often never comes because perfection is an unattainable goal.

Perfectionism also leads to paralysis by making the process of getting started feel daunting. The fear of not doing something perfectly can make any action feel insufficient. When a person believes that their work must be impeccable from the start, they can't help but freeze at the thought of not meeting their ideal standards. Even the smallest imperfection in the early stages of a project can feel like a sign of failure, causing them to hesitate or abandon the task altogether. This fear of inadequacy creates a loop of inaction—each failure, real or imagined, feeds into the desire for more preparation and refining, pushing the task further away.

Additionally, perfectionism distorts the view of progress. If someone believes that they must do everything perfectly, they may overlook small wins or the value of completing a task, no matter how imperfect. This prevents them from experiencing the sense of accomplishment and motivation that comes with progress, reinforcing the cycle of procrastination. The longer the task remains unfinished, the higher the pressure mounts, making it even more difficult to break free from the paralyzing grip of perfectionism.

The "good enough" mindset.

The "good enough" mindset is a powerful shift in perspective that encourages individuals to focus on progress and completion rather than perfection. It's about accepting that while striving for excellence is important, it's equally essential to recognize that perfection is often unattainable and that the pursuit of it can be counterproductive. Adopting this mindset can help people overcome the paralyzing effects of perfectionism and make consistent progress toward their goals.

At the core of the "good enough" mindset is the idea that doing something well, rather than perfectly, is sufficient. This mindset doesn't mean settling for mediocrity; rather, it means accepting that in many situations, perfection is neither necessary nor practical. By focusing on "good enough," individuals can take action without becoming overwhelmed by the need for flawlessness. This shift allows people to move forward, get things done, and complete tasks even if they're not perfect. In many cases, "good enough" is not only sufficient but also far more efficient than endlessly refining or perfecting something.

One of the key benefits of the "good enough" mindset is that it helps reduce anxiety and stress. Perfectionism often comes with a constant fear of failure or judgment, which can lead to procrastination and inaction. The "good enough" approach, however, removes this burden by reframing the task at hand as a stepping stone rather than a final, unchangeable product. This makes it easier to start, make mistakes, learn, and improve along the way. It encourages people to focus on progress and allows room for improvement over time, rather than expecting everything to be flawless from the outset.

Furthermore, embracing a "good enough" mindset fosters a healthier relationship with success and failure. Perfectionists often view anything less than perfect as a failure, but "good enough" allows people to see the value in completing tasks and making meaningful progress, even if the result isn't flawless. By accepting that not everything needs to be perfect, individuals can celebrate their achievements, however small, and maintain momentum without feeling like they've fallen short. This mindset shift not only boosts productivity but also enhances mental well-being by reducing the constant pressure to be flawless and instead embracing the reality that imperfection is a natural part of growth and success.

Strategies to manage high expectations.

Managing high expectations is crucial for maintaining a balanced approach to tasks, goals, and self-assessment. While having aspirations and aiming for success is important, setting expectations that are too high or unrealistic can lead to stress, burnout, and procrastination. Effectively managing high expectations involves finding a balance between ambition and realism, ensuring that goals are both challenging and achievable, while also allowing room for flexibility and imperfection.

One strategy for managing high expectations is to **break down larger goals into smaller, manageable steps**. When faced with a daunting task or an ambitious goal, it's easy to feel overwhelmed by the sheer magnitude of the challenge. By dividing a big goal into smaller, achievable milestones, you create a clear path forward. This not only makes the process feel less intimidating but also allows you to celebrate progress along the way, which can boost motivation and confidence. Achieving smaller objectives provides a sense of accomplishment and reduces the anxiety associated with trying to reach an unrealistic, all-or-nothing outcome.

Another useful strategy is to **set realistic and flexible timelines**. Often, people set deadlines or timelines based on perfectionism, expecting to complete tasks flawlessly and within a specific timeframe. However, life is unpredictable, and the pursuit of perfection can lead to frustration if things don't go according to plan. Instead of rigid deadlines, it's helpful to set more flexible, forgiving timelines that account for obstacles, delays, or the need for adjustments. This reduces the pressure of having to meet an idealized timeline and allows space for imperfections without feeling like you've failed.

Additionally, it's essential to **reframe your mindset around failure**. High expectations can often result in a fear of failure, where anything less than perfect is seen as a setback. To manage this, practice seeing failure not as something to avoid but as a part of the process of growth and learning. When you approach challenges with the understanding that mistakes are inevitable, it becomes easier to manage high expectations without becoming paralyzed by the fear of imperfection. This mindset allows for greater resilience in the face of setbacks, turning failures into opportunities for learning and improvement rather than signs of incompetence or defeat.

Finally, practicing **self-compassion** is key to managing high expectations. It's easy to be overly critical of yourself when you feel that you haven't lived up to your own or others' standards. By being kind to yourself, acknowledging your efforts, and forgiving yourself for any missteps, you can reduce the emotional weight that comes with high expectations. Self-compassion involves recognizing that no one is perfect and that making mistakes or falling short is part of being human. By offering yourself the same understanding and kindness that you would offer a friend in a similar situation, you can reduce feelings of shame or frustration, which can often contribute to procrastination.

Ultimately, managing high expectations requires a blend of realistic goal-setting, a forgiving approach to progress, and a shift in how you view failure. By embracing these strategies, you can achieve your goals while maintaining a healthy balance between ambition and well-being.

Managing fear and self-doubt

Fear and self-doubt are among the most significant barriers to productivity and action, often paralyzing individuals before they even begin. These emotions stem from a deeply ingrained fear of failure, rejection, or not meeting expectations—both internal and external. While some level of fear is natural and even helpful in motivating caution and preparation, excessive fear and self-doubt can become crippling, creating a mental blockade that prevents forward progress.

Managing fear and self-doubt requires patience and practice, but it is possible to transform these barriers into opportunities for growth. By understanding the roots of these emotions and employing strategies to address them, individuals can free themselves from the grip of fear, build self-assurance, and move forward with greater clarity and purpose.

Why failure feels so daunting.

Failure often feels daunting because of the deep emotional and psychological weight society and individuals attach to it. For many, failure is not seen as an isolated event or a stepping stone for growth, but rather as a reflection of personal inadequacy or incompetence. This perception can create intense pressure to succeed, making the prospect of falling short feel overwhelming and unbearable. The fear of failure is often rooted in past experiences, societal expectations, and an innate desire to protect one's self-esteem and sense of worth.

One of the primary reasons failure feels so intimidating is the fear of judgment and rejection. People worry that failing at a task or goal will lead to criticism from others or damage their reputation. This fear can be particularly strong in environments where perfectionism or high achievement is expected. When individuals tie their self-worth to external validation, failure becomes a threat not just to their goals but to their identity. The fear of being perceived as "not good enough" or "incapable" can lead to avoidance behaviors, such as procrastination or abandoning goals altogether, as a way to shield themselves from potential judgment.

Another factor contributing to the daunting nature of failure is the human brain's negativity bias. This bias causes people to focus more on negative outcomes than positive ones, amplifying the emotional impact of potential failure. The brain tends to catastrophize, imagining worst-case scenarios where failure leads to significant loss, humiliation, or irreversible consequences. Even when these scenarios are unlikely, the fear they generate can feel very real, making it harder to take risks or step out of one's comfort zone.

Failure can also feel particularly daunting when individuals equate their performance with their self-identity. For those who view their achievements as integral to their sense of self, failing at a task can feel like a personal failure, not just a setback. This mindset creates a high-stakes environment where any mistake or shortcoming is magnified and internalized, making failure seem much more significant than it truly is. The pressure to avoid failure at all costs often leads to perfectionism, where people set unrealistically high standards for themselves, further increasing the fear of falling short.

Lastly, cultural and societal narratives around success and failure play a role in why failure feels so daunting. Society often glorifies success and downplays the messy, imperfect process that leads to it. People see the polished end results of others' achievements but rarely witness the struggles, mistakes, and failures that occurred along the way. This creates an unrealistic standard, making failure feel like an anomaly rather than a normal part of growth. As a result, individuals may feel isolated in their experiences of failure, believing that they are uniquely flawed or incapable.

Understanding why failure feels so daunting is the first step toward dismantling its power. By reframing failure as an opportunity for growth, challenging negative thought patterns, and normalizing setbacks as part of the journey, individuals can begin to see failure not as a threat but as a necessary and valuable part of personal and professional development.

Techniques for reframing negative thoughts.

Negative thoughts often act as barriers, distorting reality and creating unnecessary fear or self-doubt. These thoughts are frequently rooted in cognitive distortions, which are habitual ways of thinking that exaggerate negativity or diminish self-worth. Reframing negative thoughts involves consciously challenging these distortions and replacing them with more balanced, constructive perspectives. This process not only helps reduce mental barriers but also fosters a healthier, more resilient mindset.

One effective technique for reframing negative thoughts is recognizing and labeling them. Many negative thoughts operate automatically, slipping into our minds unnoticed. By identifying when a thought is unhelpful or overly critical, you create a mental pause that allows you to assess its validity. For example, if you think, "I always fail at this," acknowledging the exaggeration in the word "always" can help you see that the statement isn't entirely true. This step alone can diminish the emotional weight of the thought and pave the way for a more constructive internal dialogue.

Another approach is to question the evidence supporting the negative thought. Often, our minds leap to conclusions without examining whether those conclusions are justified. Ask yourself: "What proof do I have that this thought is accurate? Is there another way to interpret the situation?" For instance, if you think, "I'll never finish this project," you might recall past experiences where you overcame similar challenges, reminding yourself of your capability. Shifting your perspective to focus on your strengths and past successes can significantly weaken the grip of negative thinking.

A third technique is to replace self-critical thoughts with affirming or neutral statements. This doesn't mean ignoring reality but rather framing it in a way that acknowledges both challenges and possibilities. Instead of thinking, "I'm terrible at public speaking," you might say, "Public speaking is challenging for me, but I can improve with practice." This shift transforms a fixed, defeatist mindset into a growth-oriented one, encouraging action and persistence rather than avoidance.

Lastly, cultivating self-compassion is crucial in reframing negative thoughts. People often speak to themselves in ways they would never address a friend, being overly harsh and unforgiving. By practicing kindness and understanding toward yourself, you can soften the impact of negative thoughts and create a mental space that supports learning and growth. Remind yourself that everyone struggles and makes mistakes, and that setbacks are a natural part of progress.

Reframing negative thoughts takes practice, but with time, it becomes easier to challenge and reframe these mental habits. By doing so, you can transform unhelpful thought patterns into empowering ones, fostering a mindset that supports confidence, resilience, and productive action.

Using visualization to boost confidence.

Visualization is a mental technique that involves creating vivid, detailed images of yourself successfully achieving your goals or navigating challenging situations. This practice leverages the brain's natural ability to simulate experiences, allowing you to rehearse success in your mind before it happens. By visualizing positive outcomes and confident actions, you can reduce self-doubt, build self-assurance, and enhance your readiness to tackle real-world challenges.

The power of visualization lies in its effect on both the mind and body. When you imagine yourself performing a task successfully, your brain activates the same neural pathways involved in actual performance. This overlap creates a sense of familiarity and preparedness, as though you've already accomplished the task. For instance, if you're nervous about giving a presentation, visualizing yourself speaking confidently, engaging the audience, and answering questions smoothly can help reduce anxiety and prime you for success. The more vividly you imagine the scenario, the more effective the visualization becomes.

To maximize the benefits of visualization, it's important to focus on both the process and the outcome. Many people visualize the end result, such as receiving applause after a presentation or crossing the finish line of a race, but neglect to imagine the steps required to get there. By visualizing the process—such as organizing your thoughts, maintaining a calm demeanor, and responding effectively to challenges—you prepare yourself for the journey, not just the destination. This detailed mental rehearsal builds confidence by reinforcing your ability to handle each stage of the task.

Emotional engagement is another key element of successful visualization. It's not enough to see yourself succeeding; you need to feel the emotions associated with that success. Imagine the pride, joy, and satisfaction that come with achieving your goal. By evoking these emotions during visualization, you create a strong psychological connection between the imagined success and your real-world efforts, making the goal feel more attainable and motivating you to take action.

Visualization can also help you overcome fear and self-doubt by shifting your focus from potential failures to potential successes. Instead of dwelling on what might go wrong, you train your mind to concentrate on what can go right. This shift in focus not only boosts confidence but also reduces the mental barriers that often lead to procrastination or hesitation.

Incorporating visualization into your daily routine can have a profound impact on your confidence and productivity. Whether you spend a few minutes each morning visualizing your goals or use the technique as a pre-task ritual to calm your nerves, it serves as a powerful reminder of your capabilities and potential. Over time, visualization can help you approach challenges with greater confidence, resilience, and determination.

Eliminating distractions

Distractions are one of the primary barriers to productivity, and their presence often perpetuates the cycle of procrastination. They can manifest externally, in the form of noise, clutter, or interruptions, or internally, as intrusive thoughts, emotional unrest, or lack of focus. Understanding and addressing both types of distractions is essential to creating an environment conducive to getting things done. Eliminating distractions is not about striving for perfection or completely isolating yourself but rather about creating an environment that supports your focus and productivity. By addressing both external and internal disruptions, decluttering your workspace, and leveraging technology effectively, you can build habits that allow you to stay engaged and accomplish your goals with greater ease.

Identifying external vs. internal distractions.

Distractions come in many forms, but they can generally be categorized as external or internal, each with unique characteristics and challenges. Understanding the difference between these two types of distractions is the first step in effectively managing them and reclaiming your focus.

External distractions are the interruptions that come from outside sources. These are the physical or environmental factors that demand your attention and disrupt your workflow. Examples include a noisy office, frequent notifications from your phone, chatty coworkers, or a cluttered workspace. These distractions are often easier to recognize because they are tangible and immediately noticeable. For instance, the sound of someone talking nearby or the constant ding of an email alert makes it obvious that your attention is being pulled away. External distractions can often be mitigated by modifying your environment, such as creating a quiet workspace, using noise-canceling headphones, or setting boundaries with others during focus time.

Internal distractions, by contrast, originate from within. They are the thoughts, emotions, and mental states that interfere with your ability to stay focused. These might include worries about upcoming deadlines, feelings of self-doubt, daydreaming, or simply a lack of motivation. Unlike external distractions, internal distractions are more subtle and harder to pinpoint because they often operate beneath the surface of your conscious awareness. For example, you might find yourself checking social media not because of an external notification but because you feel overwhelmed and are subconsciously seeking an escape. Addressing internal distractions requires introspection and emotional regulation.

The interplay between external and internal distractions is significant. For example, a cluttered desk (external) might trigger feelings of stress or overwhelm (internal), further derailing your focus. Similarly, internal distractions can make you more vulnerable to external ones. When you're already feeling unfocused or anxious, you're more likely to get sidetracked by minor interruptions, like an email or a passing conversation. Recognizing this dynamic helps you understand how to tackle distractions holistically, addressing both the external environment and your internal mindset.

The key to managing distractions is to first identify their sources. External distractions are often more straightforward to manage through changes in your surroundings or routines.

Internal distractions, however, require self-awareness and the ability to recognize patterns in your thoughts and emotions. By distinguishing between these two types of distractions and understanding their root causes, you can take proactive steps to minimize their impact and create a space for sustained focus and productivity.

Decluttering your physical and mental workspace.

A cluttered workspace, whether physical or mental, can drain your energy and hinder your ability to concentrate. When your surroundings or thoughts are in disarray, your brain has to work harder to filter out irrelevant stimuli and focus on what's important. Decluttering your physical and mental workspace is not just about tidiness; it's about creating an environment—both external and internal—that supports clarity, productivity, and a sense of calm.

Your physical workspace is a reflection of your mindset and productivity habits. A messy desk piled with papers, cables, and unused items sends a signal of chaos, which can distract and overwhelm you before you even begin your tasks. By clearing unnecessary items and organizing your space, you reduce the visual distractions that compete for your attention. A clean and functional workspace allows you to focus solely on the task at hand, promoting efficiency and a sense of control. Simple actions like keeping only the essentials on your desk, ensuring proper lighting, and arranging your tools for easy access can make a significant difference in how you approach your work.

Mental clutter, on the other hand, involves the unresolved

thoughts, worries, and distractions that occupy your mind. This internal chaos can stem from an overloaded to-do list, unaddressed anxieties, or a lack of direction. Mental clutter can lead to procrastination, as it becomes harder to prioritize tasks or think clearly. Decluttering your mental space involves techniques like writing down your thoughts, organizing your goals, and breaking tasks into manageable steps. Journaling can be particularly effective in helping you offload your thoughts and gain perspective. Similarly, practicing mindfulness or meditation can quiet the noise in your mind, allowing you to approach your work with renewed focus.

Physical and mental clutter often feed into each other. A disorganized desk can exacerbate feelings of stress, while a chaotic mental state can make it harder to tackle even simple organizational tasks. Recognizing this connection is key to creating a harmonious balance between your environment and mindset. By decluttering your physical workspace, you lay the groundwork for mental clarity, and by organizing your thoughts, you find the motivation to maintain an orderly physical space.

Decluttering is not a one-time task but an ongoing process of maintaining order and clarity. By regularly assessing your physical and mental environments and addressing sources of clutter, you create a space—both external and internal—that fosters focus, productivity, and a sense of accomplishment.

Technology tools to minimize interruptions.

In today's digital age, technology has the potential to either enhance or disrupt productivity. On one hand, it provides a vast array of tools to streamline work, manage time, and stay organized; on the other, it can also serve as a constant source of interruptions. Notifications from apps, social media updates, emails, and other digital distractions can pull your attention away from your tasks, preventing you from entering a state of deep focus. However, when used effectively, technology can be a powerful ally in minimizing interruptions and boosting productivity.

One of the most useful types of technology tools is those that block or limit access to distracting websites and apps. Programs like *Freedom, Cold Turkey,* or *StayFocusd* allow you to set boundaries by blocking access to social media sites, entertainment platforms, or news outlets during work hours. This is especially valuable for those who struggle with the temptation to check their phones or browse the internet during work sessions. By using these tools, you can create a controlled online environment that keeps you from falling into distractions and helps you stay focused on your priorities.

Another valuable tool is task management software. Applications like *Trello, Asana, Todoist,* or *Notion* help you organize your tasks and manage your time. They allow you to break down projects into smaller, actionable steps, set deadlines, and track progress. This not only helps you stay organized but also reduces the mental clutter that can arise from trying to remember everything you need to do. When tasks are clearly laid out in front of you, it's easier to stay on track and avoid distractions. Additionally, many of these tools come with reminder features, ensuring that you stay on top of deadlines and important tasks without having to rely on your memory.

For those who struggle with the temptation of checking emails and messages, email management tools can be game-changers. Tools like *Boomerang* or *Inbox Pause* allow you to schedule when emails are sent or received, as well as pause incoming emails so they don't constantly disrupt your workflow. This helps create periods of focused work where you aren't constantly reacting to incoming messages. Setting specific times to check and respond to emails, rather than allowing them to interrupt your day at random intervals, enables you to focus on more critical tasks without feeling overwhelmed by constant notifications.

For those who need to structure their time and maintain focus, productivity timers like the *Pomodoro Technique* can be incredibly useful. Apps such as *Focus Booster* or *Be Focused* allow you to break your work into intervals, typically 25 minutes of focused work followed by a short break. This technique not only helps maintain your focus but also prevents burnout by encouraging regular rest. Having a timer can be a great way to limit distractions and ensure that you're staying productive during work sessions.

Additionally, there are apps specifically designed for maintaining mental focus and minimizing distractions. *Forest*, for example, rewards you for staying focused by growing a virtual tree while you work. If you leave the app to check your phone, the tree withers. This gamified element provides an incentive to stay focused and discourages mindless scrolling. Similarly, *Focus@Will* offers music and soundscapes designed to enhance concentration and block out distractions, creating an auditory environment conducive to deep work.

Incorporating these technology tools into your workflow can significantly reduce interruptions and help you maintain focus throughout the day. However, it's important to remember that technology is most effective when combined with a strong sense of self-discipline. While these tools can help create boundaries, the key to staying productive lies in your ability to manage your time and attention effectively. By leveraging technology strategically, you can reduce distractions and create an environment that supports your goals.

5

TIME MANAGEMENT FOR THE MODERN PROCRASTINATOR

Prioritization strategies

Prioritization is one of the most crucial aspects of overcoming procrastination because it helps you focus on what truly matters rather than getting caught up in less significant tasks. Without a clear sense of priority, it's easy to become overwhelmed by the sheer number of things you need to do, which can lead to procrastination or burnout. Prioritizing effectively allows you to take control of your time, energy, and efforts, ensuring that you're consistently working on the most important things that align with your personal and professional goals.

At the core of prioritization lies the ability to distinguish between what is urgent and what is important. Urgent tasks often come with deadlines or external pressure, making them feel immediate and demanding. However, not all urgent tasks are critical to your long-term success. On the other hand, important tasks are those that contribute to your larger goals, but they don't always carry the same time-sensitive urgency. The challenge is in recognizing which tasks fall into each category and then managing your time accordingly, so you don't get bogged down by tasks that, while urgent, don't actually move you closer to your bigger objectives.

One strategy that can help you manage priorities more effectively is the Eisenhower Matrix. This tool helps you categorize tasks into four distinct quadrants based on their urgency and importance. By separating tasks in this way, you can avoid wasting time on less important tasks and focus your attention on what truly moves the needle. The idea is to eliminate or delegate tasks that are neither urgent nor important, address the important but non-urgent tasks before they become urgent, and deal with urgent tasks in a way that doesn't distract from your long-term goals.

Another important aspect of prioritization is aligning your tasks with your long-term goals. It's easy to become side-tracked by daily distractions and short-term demands, but to make lasting progress, you must ensure that what you're working on is in line with your bigger vision. This requires taking the time to clearly define your long-term objectives and then breaking them down into smaller, actionable steps. These smaller steps can then be prioritized within your daily or weekly to-do lists, ensuring that you're consistently moving forward toward your bigger ambitions.

When you master prioritization, you not only improve your efficiency and productivity but also reduce the mental clutter that comes from feeling overwhelmed by a mountain of tasks.

By learning to prioritize effectively, you take charge of your time and energy, allowing you to move through your day with greater focus and purpose, and ultimately, to defeat procrastination. Prioritization doesn't just help you decide what to do; it helps you choose what not to do, ensuring that your efforts are always aligned with your long-term goals and that you're making meaningful progress toward achieving them.

The Eisenhower Matrix.

The Eisenhower Matrix is a powerful tool for prioritizing tasks based on urgency and importance. Named after U.S. President Dwight D. Eisenhower, who famously said, "What is important is seldom urgent, and what is urgent is seldom important," this matrix helps individuals identify and focus on the tasks that truly matter. The matrix divides tasks into four categories: urgent and important, not urgent but important, urgent but not important, and neither urgent nor important.

By categorizing tasks in this way, you can quickly assess where your energy should be directed. Tasks that fall into the "urgent and important" quadrant require immediate attention and should be prioritized above all else. These are often the tasks that have deadlines or consequences if not addressed promptly. On the other hand, tasks that are "not urgent but important" are the ones that contribute to long-term goals and growth. These are the activities that require careful planning and sustained effort over time.

The third category—"urgent but not important"—includes tasks that may demand immediate attention but are not crucial to your long-term objectives. These are often distractions or requests from others that you feel obligated to handle immediately but can often be delegated or rescheduled. Finally, tasks that fall into the "neither urgent nor important" quadrant can typically be eliminated or deferred entirely, as they don't contribute meaningfully to your goals. By using the Eisenhower Matrix, you gain clarity on what to focus on, what to delegate, and what to let go of, allowing you to allocate your time and energy more effectively.

How to distinguish between urgent and important.

One of the key concepts behind the Eisenhower Matrix is understanding the difference between urgent and important tasks. Urgency refers to tasks that demand immediate attention, often with looming deadlines or external pressures. These are the tasks that feel like they can't wait, such as responding to emails, attending meetings, or handling last-minute requests. However, just because something is urgent doesn't mean it is important.

Importance, on the other hand, refers to tasks that contribute to long-term goals, personal growth, or major life objectives. These tasks often don't come with immediate deadlines, which can make them easier to overlook or procrastinate on. For example, writing a book, pursuing further education, or building a new skill might not have pressing deadlines, but they are crucial for your long-term success and happiness.

Distinguishing between the two involves taking a step back and evaluating the broader impact of each task. Urgent tasks often come from external pressures, such as others' needs or immediate situations, while important tasks tend to align with your personal values and long-term goals. To help identify which tasks fall into which category, ask yourself questions like: "Will completing this task help me achieve my larger goals?" or "Will this task have lasting consequences if not addressed now?"

Aligning tasks with long-term goals.

One of the most effective prioritization strategies is aligning your daily tasks with your long-term goals. Often, it's easy to get caught up in the whirlwind of urgent tasks that feel pressing but don't actually contribute to our overarching objectives. Aligning tasks with your long-term goals helps ensure that your actions are purposeful and directed toward meaningful achievements.

The first step in aligning your tasks is to clearly define your long-term goals. What do you hope to achieve in the next year, five years, or even a decade? Once these goals are clearly identified, break them down into smaller, actionable steps that can be incorporated into your daily tasks. For example, if one of your long-term goals is to become financially independent, breaking that down into tasks like creating a budget, saving a certain percentage of your income, and researching investment strategies will help you align your daily actions with that larger vision.

Aligning tasks with long-term goals also means saying no to distractions and non-essential tasks that don't serve your objectives. Regularly evaluate whether the tasks on your to-do list are moving you toward your goals or merely serving to fill up your time. This helps you avoid the trap of busywork and ensures that you are consistently making progress in areas that matter most. By prioritizing tasks that are aligned with your long-term goals, you create a sense of purpose and direction in your work, which can increase motivation and reduce procrastination.

The power of scheduling

Scheduling is one of the most powerful tools for overcoming procrastination because it transforms vague intentions into actionable plans. It's not enough to know what needs to be done; deciding when to do it is just as critical. When you assign specific times to tasks, you create structure and accountability, reducing the chances of putting things off indefinitely. Scheduling helps you prioritize effectively, manage your time, and maintain a steady workflow, even when life gets busy or distractions arise. The power of scheduling lies in its ability to turn abstract goals into tangible steps. When you plan your time intentionally, you take control of your day rather than letting it control you. It's not just about getting things done but about creating a rhythm that aligns with your energy levels, priorities, and long-term aspirations. With a well-structured schedule, you can work smarter, stay motivated, and make meaningful progress, all while keeping procrastination at bay.

Why "when" matters as much as "what."

The timing of tasks, or the "when," is as crucial as deciding "what" to do because the time you choose to act significantly impacts your energy, focus, and productivity. It's not just about having a to-do list; it's about strategically planning when each task fits best into your day to maximize efficiency and success. Our bodies and minds operate on natural rhythms, and understanding these cycles can help us work with them rather than against them.

Every person experiences fluctuations in energy and mental clarity throughout the day, often referred to as their circadian rhythm. For many, peak productivity occurs in the morning, when energy levels are high, and distractions are fewer. This makes it an ideal time to tackle tasks that require deep concentration, problem-solving, or creativity. On the other hand, afternoons might lend themselves better to lighter, more routine tasks as focus begins to wane. By aligning your tasks with your natural energy peaks and troughs, you can make the most of your productive hours and avoid unnecessary procrastination.

Another reason timing is critical is the concept of decision fatigue. As the day progresses, the mental effort required to make choices accumulates, leaving you less capable of effectively prioritizing or taking action. Scheduling high-priority or demanding tasks earlier in the day can help ensure they get done when your decision-making ability is at its sharpest. By contrast, leaving important tasks for later often results in procrastination as your mental resources become depleted.

External factors also play a role in the importance of timing.

Tasks often have dependencies, deadlines, or ideal conditions for completion. Understanding these factors can help you set realistic timeframes and avoid bottlenecks. For instance, scheduling collaborative tasks during times when team members are available ensures smoother communication and progress. Similarly, knowing when interruptions are likely to occur can help you plan focused work sessions during quieter periods.

Choosing the right "when" not only improves your productivity but also reduces stress. Instead of constantly reacting to whatever comes your way, a well-planned schedule allows you to anticipate challenges and allocate time accordingly. It creates a sense of control and flow, turning even a busy day into one that feels manageable and purposeful. By focusing on when to do something as much as what to do, you position yourself for success and significantly reduce the likelihood of procrastination.

Time blocking and calendar mastery.

Time blocking and calendar mastery are transformative strategies for managing your time and boosting productivity. Together, they provide a structured framework for organizing your day, ensuring that your priorities are addressed without being overshadowed by distractions or less important tasks.

Time blocking is the practice of dividing your day into segments, each dedicated to a specific task or category of activity. Instead of simply creating a to-do list, you allocate fixed periods to each task on your schedule. For example, you might reserve two hours in the morning for deep work, thirty minutes for email, and an hour in the afternoon for a meeting.

By assigning precise time slots to your tasks, you minimize the guesswork of deciding what to do next and reduce the temptation to procrastinate. Time blocking also forces you to confront the reality of how much time you actually have, promoting more realistic planning and better prioritization.

Calendar mastery takes time blocking a step further by turning your calendar into a visual representation of your intentions, commitments, and goals. A well-maintained calendar not only reflects what needs to be done but also when and how you'll accomplish it. By regularly reviewing and updating your calendar, you gain a clear understanding of your obligations and available time, helping you avoid overcommitting or neglecting important tasks. Digital calendars, with features like reminders and recurring events, make it easier than ever to manage your schedule effectively and ensure that nothing falls through the cracks.

One of the key benefits of time blocking and calendar mastery is their ability to help you focus. When you know exactly what you should be working on at any given moment, you can eliminate the mental clutter of juggling competing demands. This focused approach reduces decision fatigue and allows you to channel your energy into meaningful work. Additionally, time blocking encourages balance by ensuring that all areas of your life—work, health, relationships, and leisure—are accounted for in your schedule.

Another advantage is flexibility. While time blocking may seem rigid, it actually allows you to adapt more easily to unexpected changes. If an urgent issue arises, you can see at a glance what can be rescheduled or shifted without losing sight of your overall priorities. Calendar mastery helps you stay agile, ensuring that disruptions don't derail your entire day.

By mastering time blocking and your calendar, you move from a reactive approach to time management to a proactive one. You take control of your hours and days, making intentional choices about how to spend your time. This level of organization not only boosts productivity but also provides a sense of accomplishment and peace of mind, making it easier to overcome procrastination and achieve your goals.

Creating buffers for unexpected delays.

Creating buffers for unexpected delays is a crucial time management strategy that allows you to navigate disruptions without derailing your schedule or increasing stress. Life is inherently unpredictable, and even the most well-planned days can be interrupted by unforeseen events, such as technical issues, last-minute requests, or simply tasks taking longer than expected. By building extra time into your schedule, you create a cushion that absorbs these disruptions and helps you stay on track.

A buffer is essentially a block of unscheduled time intentionally left open between tasks or activities. Instead of planning your day with back-to-back commitments, you leave room for flexibility. For example, if you estimate a task will take an hour, you might schedule an additional 15–30 minutes as a buffer. This ensures that even if the task overruns, you won't immediately fall behind on subsequent tasks. Buffers are particularly valuable for complex or unpredictable tasks, where underestimating the time required is common.

Buffers also serve as a psychological safety net. Knowing you have extra time built into your schedule reduces the pressure to complete everything perfectly or as quickly as possible. This sense of control can improve focus and reduce procrastination, as you're less likely to avoid tasks out of fear of failure or time constraints. Instead, you can approach your work with confidence, knowing you have room to adjust if needed.

Moreover, buffers help you manage transitions between activities. Shifting from one task to another often requires mental or physical preparation, whether it's gathering materials, resetting your focus, or traveling to a different location. Without adequate time for these transitions, you may find yourself rushing, which can lead to mistakes or frustration. Buffers allow for smoother, less stressful shifts between tasks, contributing to a more productive and enjoyable day.

Another advantage of buffers is their role in maintaining work-life balance. By accounting for unexpected delays, you're less likely to carry over unfinished work into your personal time. Buffers can act as a boundary, ensuring that your schedule doesn't overflow and encroach on moments meant for relaxation or family. This balance is essential for long-term productivity and well-being.

Creating effective buffers requires self-awareness and realistic planning. It's important to understand your tendencies—such as whether you often underestimate task durations—and adjust your buffer times accordingly. While it may seem counterintuitive to "waste" time by not scheduling every minute, buffers actually make your schedule more efficient and sustainable. They provide the flexibility and resilience needed to handle the unexpected, ultimately helping you stay productive, calm, and in control.

Overcoming decision fatigue

Overcoming decision fatigue is an essential step toward maintaining productivity and mental clarity in a world filled with endless choices. Decision fatigue occurs when the quality of our decisions deteriorates after making too many choices over time. Every decision, no matter how small, requires mental energy, and as the day progresses, this energy becomes depleted. This phenomenon can lead to procrastination, impulsive decisions, or avoidance altogether, which can derail even the most well-intentioned plans. By addressing decision fatigue through simplification, routines, and automation, you create an environment where your mental energy is preserved for the decisions that truly matter. This not only helps you stay productive but also reduces stress and enhances overall well-being. Taking control of decision fatigue isn't just about efficiency—it's about reclaiming the mental clarity and focus needed to achieve your goals.

Simplifying your choices.

Simplifying your choices is a powerful method for reducing mental fatigue and increasing productivity. Every choice, no matter how small, demands cognitive effort. Over time, the accumulation of these decisions can lead to a phenomenon called decision fatigue, where the quality of our choices diminishes. Simplification reduces the mental burden by narrowing down options, enabling you to focus your energy on more important matters.

A key aspect of simplifying choices is minimizing the number of decisions you need to make in your daily life. This can involve pre-planning or systematizing repetitive tasks. For instance, choosing your meals for the week or laying out your clothes the night before eliminates the need for daily deliberation. By establishing these habits, you free up mental space for more complex or creative thinking. Simplifying doesn't mean sacrificing quality but rather being intentional and deliberate about the choices that truly matter.

Another effective strategy is setting clear priorities. When you know what's most important, you can eliminate less significant options without hesitation. This approach prevents analysis paralysis, where overthinking slows progress. For example, when faced with a long to-do list, focusing on your top three priorities ensures you channel your energy effectively without getting bogged down by lesser tasks. By streamlining decision-making in this way, you avoid the exhaustion of constantly weighing pros and cons.

Simplifying choices also involves creating boundaries that limit distractions and unnecessary options. In today's world, we're bombarded with endless possibilities, from entertainment to consumer products. Setting limits, such as only watching one show at a time or unsubscribing from irrelevant notifications, reduces the clutter that competes for your attention. This intentional narrowing of options not only makes decision-making easier but also enhances satisfaction with the choices you do make.

Ultimately, simplifying choices is about valuing your time and mental energy. It's a way of reclaiming control over your day and focusing on what truly matters to you. By reducing the number of trivial decisions, you create room for the ones that can have a meaningful impact on your goals and overall well-being.

Setting up routines to reduce mental load.

Setting up routines to reduce mental load is a transformative approach to enhancing productivity and conserving mental energy. Routines eliminate the need to make frequent decisions about recurring tasks, allowing your brain to operate on autopilot for predictable parts of your day. By reducing the mental effort required for basic activities, you can reserve cognitive resources for more important and demanding tasks.

A well-designed routine creates structure and predictability in your day. When you establish a consistent pattern for activities like waking up, exercising, or planning your day, you minimize the need to decide when and how to do these things. This predictability frees you from the mental strain of constantly figuring out what comes next. For example, starting your morning with a set sequence—such as drinking water, meditating, and reviewing your goals—sets a positive tone for the day while conserving energy for more complex decisions later.

Routines also reduce the likelihood of procrastination. When tasks are part of a habitual sequence, there's less opportunity to delay or debate whether to do them. For instance, if you consistently write for 30 minutes every evening, it becomes a natural part of your schedule rather than an activity you must decide on daily. Over time, routines build momentum and reinforce discipline, making it easier to maintain focus and achieve long-term goals.

Another benefit of routines is their ability to provide mental clarity by removing decision clutter. Without a routine, small decisions—like what to eat for breakfast or when to work out—can accumulate and drain your mental energy before you tackle bigger challenges. By automating these choices, you preserve your decision-making capacity for more critical matters. Additionally, routines can help you transition smoothly between tasks, reducing the mental effort required to shift focus.

Setting up routines also instills a sense of control and stability, especially during periods of uncertainty. When external circumstances are chaotic, a consistent routine provides an anchor, helping you stay grounded and productive. Whether it's a nightly wind-down ritual to improve sleep or a dedicated block of time for creative work, routines give your day a framework that supports efficiency and peace of mind.

Ultimately, routines are not about rigidity but about creating a reliable system that supports your goals and reduces unnecessary stress. By streamlining your daily actions into habits, you simplify your life and empower yourself to focus on what truly matters.

Automating repetitive tasks.

Automating repetitive tasks is a practical and highly effective way to save time, conserve mental energy, and increase overall efficiency. Repetitive tasks, though often simple, consume a disproportionate amount of attention when performed manually. By automating these actions, you can shift your focus to more meaningful and strategic work while ensuring routine responsibilities are handled consistently and reliably.

Automation removes the need for constant decision-making or manual intervention. Tasks like paying bills, scheduling social media posts, or managing email can be automated using tools and systems designed for these purposes. For instance, setting up automatic payments for monthly expenses eliminates the need to remember deadlines, reducing stress and the chance of late fees. Similarly, using email filters to sort incoming messages into folders or mark certain emails as important streamlines communication and prevents inbox overwhelm.

A significant advantage of automation is the reduction of human error. When repetitive tasks are performed manually, mistakes are more likely due to fatigue or distraction. Automating these tasks ensures accuracy and consistency, as the process is performed by a system that follows predetermined rules. This is especially valuable for tasks like data entry, reporting, or inventory management, where errors can be costly and time-consuming to fix.

Automation also allows you to scale your efforts. For example, in professional settings, marketing campaigns, customer service inquiries, or content distribution can be managed through automated platforms. Tools like CRM systems or workflow software handle large volumes of tasks efficiently, enabling you to achieve more without increasing your workload. On a personal level, apps that track fitness goals, send reminders, or suggest meal plans can simplify daily living and keep you on track with minimal effort.

Implementing automation may require an initial investment of time and effort to set up the necessary systems. However, this upfront work quickly pays off by saving hours of manual labor in the long run. For instance, creating templates for repetitive emails or configuring smart home devices to control lighting and appliances can significantly reduce daily decision-making. Over time, the cumulative effect of these small efficiencies translates to a substantial boost in productivity.

Automation is not about eliminating human involvement entirely but about delegating mundane and repetitive tasks to technology so that your attention is freed for creative, strategic, and high-priority activities. By leveraging automation, you create a workflow that is not only efficient but also allows you to focus on what matters most, making your life and work more manageable and fulfilling.

6

REWIRING YOUR BRAIN FOR PRODUCTIVITY

Neuroplasticity and habit formation

Neuroplasticity and habit formation are deeply interconnected processes that reveal the brain's incredible ability to adapt and transform over time. At its core, neuroplasticity refers to the brain's capacity to reorganize itself by forming new neural connections. This remarkable feature of the brain underpins our ability to create habits, break old ones, and adopt new patterns of behavior. Understanding this dynamic process can empower individuals to take control of their actions and shape their lives more intentionally. Ultimately, the principles of neuroplasticity and habit formation remind us that change is always possible, no matter how entrenched a behavior may seem. By understanding the science behind these processes and applying

74

deliberate strategies, individuals can reshape their habits, behaviors, and even their identities. This journey requires patience and persistence, but the rewards—greater control, productivity, and fulfillment—are well worth the effort.

How habits shape behavior over time.

Habits shape behavior over time by creating automatic patterns of action that streamline decision-making and conserve mental energy. Once established, habits operate below conscious awareness, guiding our choices and responses without requiring deliberate thought. This efficiency is both the strength and the challenge of habits: they enable consistency and reliability but can also perpetuate behaviors that may not align with our goals.

At the core of this process is the brain's preference for predictability and routine. The more a behavior is repeated, the stronger the neural pathways associated with that action become. Over time, these pathways form a kind of default setting for the brain, making the habit easier to execute and harder to change. For instance, brushing your teeth or tying your shoes involves little to no conscious effort because the brain has encoded these actions into a well-worn neural groove.

Habits also shape behavior by creating feedback loops that reinforce their existence. When a habit is performed, it often results in a reward—whether tangible, like a treat, or intangible, like a sense of accomplishment. This reward strengthens the habit loop, making it more likely the behavior will be repeated. For example, if you habitually exercise and experience a rush of endorphins afterward, your brain registers this positive outcome and encourages you to exercise again. Conversely, habits formed around negative rewards, such as stress relief from procrastination, can entrench behaviors that ultimately work against you.

The cumulative impact of habits over time can be profound. A single habit, repeated daily, has the potential to significantly influence a person's trajectory. Consider the habit of reading for 15 minutes every evening. While it may seem small in isolation, over a year, this amounts to several books read, which could lead to enhanced knowledge, improved focus, or personal growth. Similarly, negative habits, like excessive screen time before bed, may gradually erode sleep quality, impacting energy levels, productivity, and overall well-being.

Habits also interact with one another, creating a ripple effect that can amplify their influence. A positive habit in one area, such as starting a morning routine, can trigger other productive behaviors, like eating a healthy breakfast or planning your day effectively. This phenomenon, often called habit stacking, illustrates how small changes can compound over time to produce transformative results.

The power of habits lies in their ability to persist long after the initial effort to establish them. While forming a new habit requires intentionality and discipline, the eventual payoff is a behavior that becomes second nature. This is why understanding how habits shape behavior over time is crucial: it enables you to harness their potential to create a life aligned with your values and goals. Whether working to build positive habits or break unhelpful ones, the time and effort invested in understanding and shaping your habits is an investment in your future self.

Replacing old habits with new, productive ones.

Replacing old habits with new, productive ones is a process of intentional change that requires both commitment and strategy. It's not just about quitting a negative behavior but actively replacing it with something that serves your greater goals. Old habits, especially those that are deeply ingrained, have a powerful grip on the brain because they've been reinforced over time. To break free from these, you need to disrupt the old pattern and introduce a new one that offers similar benefits but in a more constructive way.

The first step in replacing old habits is recognizing the triggers that lead to the undesired behavior. Triggers can be environmental cues, emotional states, or certain situations that prompt automatic reactions. For example, if stress leads you to procrastinate, identifying this trigger allows you to intervene before the habit takes over. The goal is to interrupt the cycle of the old habit and replace it with an alternative behavior that is aligned with your long-term objectives. This requires conscious effort, as the brain is initially resistant to change. However, with time and repetition, the new behavior can become just as automatic as the old one.

One of the most effective methods for replacing old habits is habit stacking. This involves pairing the new habit with an existing behavior that is already established. For instance, if you want to develop the habit of exercising in the morning, you might stack it with the habit of having coffee. After you brew your morning coffee, you could immediately engage in a brief workout. Over time, the association between these two actions will make it easier to perform the new behavior. The key here is consistency; the more you repeat the new habit in conjunction with an established one, the more likely it is to stick.

It's also important to make the new habit rewarding. The brain tends to favor behaviors that result in positive outcomes, so making the new habit satisfying in some way increases the chances of its success. If your goal is to start a journaling habit, for example, you might reward yourself with a small treat or allow yourself to unwind with a favorite activity after writing. This reinforcement creates a positive feedback loop that strengthens the new behavior and makes it feel more rewarding than the old habit.

Moreover, it's crucial to practice patience and self-compassion throughout this process. Replacing old habits is rarely instantaneous. It takes time for the new behavior to become automatic, and setbacks are a normal part of the journey. Rather than feeling discouraged by occasional failures, it's important to acknowledge progress and keep refining the new habit until it feels natural. As you continue to practice the new habit, it will gradually replace the old one, and the neural pathways associated with the previous behavior will begin to weaken.

Finally, the environment plays a significant role in this process. Making small changes to your environment to support the new habit can reinforce your efforts. If you're trying to eat healthier, for example, keeping junk food out of sight and stocking your kitchen with nutritious options can make it easier to adopt the new behavior. By altering your surroundings to encourage the new habit, you minimize the temptation to fall back into old patterns.

Ultimately, replacing old habits with new, productive ones is a transformative process that requires a combination of awareness, strategy, and persistence. By identifying triggers, pairing behaviors, making the new habit rewarding, and staying patient, you can reshape your habits in a way that aligns with your long-term goals and enhances your overall well-being. The power of neuroplasticity ensures that with time and effort, new behaviors can become as automatic as the old, and lasting change is within your reach.

The power of tiny, consistent changes.

The power of tiny, consistent changes lies in their ability to accumulate over time, leading to significant transformation with minimal effort at the outset. This concept is rooted in the principle of compounding, where small, seemingly insignificant actions build upon each other to produce remarkable results. Rather than attempting a drastic overhaul, focusing on small, manageable changes allows for sustainable progress and reduces the overwhelm that often accompanies large, ambitious goals.

When you commit to making tiny changes consistently, you create a ripple effect that gradually reshapes your behavior. These changes, though small in the beginning, are easier to implement and maintain because they don't demand a huge amount of energy or motivation. This makes it more likely that you will stick with them, even when life gets busy or challenging. For example, if your goal is to get fit, starting with just five minutes of exercise a day may seem minimal, but doing it every day will establish a routine. Over time, the duration and intensity of your workouts can naturally increase as you become more comfortable and confident in your ability to stick with the habit.

Consistency plays a crucial role in this process. It's the repeated action over time that creates lasting change, not one-off efforts. The key is to ensure that each small step you take is aligned with your end goal. As you repeat these tiny changes, they begin to reinforce each other and create a sense of momentum. This momentum is powerful because it propels you forward, making it easier to continue and expand your efforts. The more consistent you are, the more ingrained the new behavior becomes, eventually transforming it into a habit that feels natural.

Tiny, consistent changes also reduce the risk of burnout or failure. When people attempt drastic changes all at once, they often face a period of intense effort followed by a drop-off when they become overwhelmed or discouraged. With small changes, the pressure is lower, and the process feels more manageable. This steady progress fosters a sense of accomplishment and builds confidence, creating a positive feedback loop that encourages further action.

In addition to being manageable, tiny changes are less intimidating because they don't require a large leap outside of your comfort zone. By starting small, you avoid the all-or-nothing mentality that often leads to procrastination. Each small success, no matter how minor it seems, reinforces the belief that change is possible, making it easier to continue. For instance, if your goal is to read more books, starting with reading just one page a day can eventually lead to finishing a book every week or month, without the pressure of setting a lofty goal from the start.

The cumulative impact of tiny, consistent changes can be transformative in many areas of life. Whether it's building a new skill, improving health, or developing a productive routine, focusing on incremental progress allows you to steadily move closer to your desired outcome without feeling overwhelmed. This approach is not only more sustainable but also more forgiving, as small setbacks are easier to recover from and don't derail the overall progress.

In essence, the power of tiny, consistent changes is about making progress that feels achievable and maintaining it over time. By embracing small actions, staying consistent, and celebrating the incremental wins, you can create lasting change without the burnout or frustration that often accompanies big, sudden shifts. It's through these small steps that great transformations unfold, proving that slow and steady can indeed win the race.

The role of mindfulness

Mindfulness is a powerful tool that can significantly reduce procrastination by helping individuals become more aware of their thoughts, emotions, and behaviors in the present moment. When you practice mindfulness, you become more attuned to your tendencies, including the moments when procrastination sets in. By observing these tendencies without judgment, you can interrupt the cycle of avoidance and redirect your focus toward the task at hand. Mindfulness encourages non-reactivity, which means you can recognize feelings of resistance or distraction without automatically acting on them. This allows you to make more conscious decisions about how to proceed with tasks instead of falling into the trap of putting them off.

How mindfulness reduces procrastination.

Mindfulness reduces procrastination by fostering a heightened awareness of the present moment and enabling individuals to observe their thoughts, emotions, and behaviors without judgment. Procrastination often arises from internal resistance, anxiety, or distractions, and mindfulness allows you to become aware of these underlying triggers before they spiral out of control. By practicing mindfulness, you can observe procrastination as it arises, and rather than reacting impulsively to avoid the task, you can consciously choose how to respond.

When you're mindful, you're less likely to fall into patterns of avoidance or procrastination because you're able to acknowledge the discomfort that may come with starting a task without immediately succumbing to it. Mindfulness provides a mental space between your thoughts and actions, which creates the opportunity to decide whether to engage with the task or not. This awareness helps you detach from automatic thoughts like "I'll do it later" or "This is too difficult," allowing you to face the task with greater clarity and intention.

Additionally, mindfulness reduces procrastination by promoting a non-judgmental attitude. Often, we procrastinate because of fear of failure, perfectionism, or self-doubt. When we view our tasks through a lens of judgment, they become sources of anxiety, making us reluctant to start. Mindfulness encourages you to approach tasks without labeling them as "good" or "bad" but simply as actions to be completed. This non-judgmental mindset lowers the stakes of starting a task, making it less intimidating and more approachable.

By focusing on the present moment, mindfulness also helps

you let go of future worries and distractions, which often fuel procrastination. Instead of getting overwhelmed by the "what-ifs" and potential consequences of your work, mindfulness brings you back to the now, where you can simply engage with the task at hand, one step at a time. This focus on immediate action prevents you from mentally spiraling into a cycle of delay.

Moreover, mindfulness promotes self-compassion, which is key in overcoming procrastination. Instead of beating yourself up for procrastinating, mindfulness encourages a gentle, understanding approach to your habits. This reduces the feelings of guilt or shame that often accompany procrastination, which can further contribute to avoidance. By cultivating a more compassionate inner dialogue, mindfulness helps you take action without the emotional burden that typically holds you back.

Ultimately, mindfulness helps you break free from the automatic, reactive patterns that lead to procrastination, allowing you to approach your tasks with a clearer, calmer mind and a greater sense of agency. It empowers you to engage with the present moment, reducing the need for avoidance and allowing you to make more deliberate and productive choices.

Techniques to stay present and focused.

Staying present and focused can be challenging, especially with the constant barrage of distractions in our modern world. However, there are several techniques that can help sharpen your attention and keep you grounded in the present moment, ultimately boosting your productivity and reducing procrastination. These techniques are rooted in mindfulness practices, which train your mind to focus on the task at hand and avoid getting lost in distractions or negative thought loops.

One effective technique is the **body scan**. This practice involves mentally scanning your body from head to toe, paying close attention to any sensations you might feel. It helps bring your awareness back to the present moment by connecting you with the physical reality of your body. When you notice your mind wandering or when you begin to feel overwhelmed, you can use a body scan to refocus. By grounding yourself in bodily sensations, you redirect your attention from unproductive thoughts to your immediate experience. This is especially helpful when you're finding it difficult to stay focused on a task.

Another technique to stay present and focused is **breath awareness**. Simply focusing on your breath can quickly center your mind and pull it away from distractions. You can practice mindful breathing by paying attention to the sensation of air entering and exiting your nostrils or noticing the rise and fall of your chest or abdomen. When your mind begins to wander, gently bring it back to your breath without judgment. This act of refocusing is a simple but powerful way to regain control of your attention and stay present in the moment.

Single-tasking is another technique that combats the modern tendency to multitask, which can scatter your attention and diminish productivity. When working on a task, dedicate your full attention to it rather than trying to juggle multiple tasks at once. Research has shown that multitasking reduces efficiency and increases cognitive overload. By committing to one task at a time, you can deepen your focus and perform more effectively. If you find yourself tempted to check your phone or shift to another task, gently remind yourself to bring your focus back to the task at hand.

Setting specific intentions before starting a task can also help you stay present and focused. Rather than diving into a project with a vague sense of purpose, set a clear intention for what you want to accomplish. This can be as simple as stating, "I will write 500 words in the next 30 minutes," or "I will finish this email by the end of this session." Having a clear goal in mind not only helps you stay focused but also gives you a sense of purpose and motivation to continue working. It's important to review your intention periodically during your work session to stay on track.

Mindful breaks are crucial for maintaining sustained focus throughout the day. Taking short, purposeful breaks can help reset your mind and prevent burnout. A break doesn't have to mean complete disengagement—consider doing something like stretching, walking, or taking a few deep breaths. The key is to break the mental cycle of focus in a healthy way so that when you return to your task, you feel refreshed and ready to continue.

Lastly, **eliminating distractions** is an essential technique to staying present. This includes both external distractions, like noise or notifications, and internal distractions, such as wandering thoughts or worries. You can minimize external distractions by creating a dedicated workspace, turning off notifications, or using apps that block distracting websites during work sessions. For internal distractions, mindfulness techniques like breath awareness or body scans can help you gently refocus when your thoughts drift away from the task.

By incorporating these techniques into your routine, you can train your mind to stay present and focused, ultimately increasing your productivity and reducing the temptation to procrastinate. It's important to remember that staying focused is a skill that takes time to develop. Regular practice will help strengthen your ability to maintain attention, reduce distractions, and keep procrastination at bay.

Building a meditation practice for productivity.

Building a meditation practice for productivity involves using mindfulness techniques to enhance focus, clarity, and mental resilience, all of which contribute to improved productivity. Meditation, when practiced regularly, helps train the mind to stay present, reduce stress, and improve cognitive function, all of which are essential for overcoming procrastination and getting things done efficiently.

To start building a meditation practice, it's important to begin with **short sessions** and gradually increase the duration as you become more comfortable with the practice. Even just five to ten minutes of meditation each day can yield significant benefits. These short sessions can help clear mental clutter, calm your nervous system, and prepare you to focus on tasks with greater intention and awareness. It's essential to view meditation not as an extra task on your to-do list but as a tool that directly enhances your productivity by creating a more centered, focused mind.

Breath-focused meditation is a great starting point. By simply focusing on your breath, you can bring your attention back to the present moment, reducing the distractions that often lead to procrastination. The practice involves sitting in a comfortable position and focusing on the sensation of your breath as it moves in and out of your body. If your mind starts to wander, gently guide it back to your breath without judgment. This simple practice helps train the mind to return to focus whenever it drifts, which is a crucial skill for productivity.

Another useful meditation technique for productivity is **guided meditation**. Guided meditation involves following a pre-recorded session, usually led by an instructor who provides instructions and prompts throughout the session. These sessions often focus on themes like relaxation, focus, or visualization, which can help sharpen your concentration and energize your mind for the tasks ahead. Guided meditation can be particularly helpful for beginners, as it provides structure and direction, making it easier to maintain focus during the practice.

Once you feel more comfortable with meditation, you can explore **mindfulness meditation**, which involves paying attention to your thoughts, feelings, and sensations without judgment. In the context of productivity, mindfulness meditation helps you become aware of procrastination triggers—such as negative thoughts, doubts, or distractions—before they lead to delay. By acknowledging these thoughts in a non-reactive way, you can choose not to engage with them and instead stay focused on the task at hand.

To make meditation a regular habit, it's helpful to integrate it into your daily routine. You might choose to meditate first thing in the morning to set a positive tone for the day, or you could use meditation as a mid-day break to reset your mind and recharge. **Consistency is key**, so it's important to stick with the practice even if it feels challenging at first. Over time, meditation can help you build a greater sense of clarity, focus, and emotional regulation, which are all essential for sustained productivity.

Body scan meditation is another powerful technique for productivity. This practice involves mentally scanning your body, paying attention to each part and noticing any tension or discomfort. The body scan helps release stress and promotes a sense of calm, which can improve mental clarity and focus. By regularly practicing body scans, you train your mind to recognize when you're holding stress or tension, allowing you to release it and refocus on your tasks.

Meditation also plays a significant role in developing **emotional resilience**. The more you meditate, the more you become aware of your emotions and how they influence your behavior. For example, you may notice that procrastination often arises when you're feeling overwhelmed or anxious about a task. Meditation helps you observe these emotional triggers without reacting to them, allowing you to handle challenges with a calmer, more composed mindset. This emotional regulation is essential for maintaining focus and productivity over time.

Finally, **visualization techniques** can be incorporated into your meditation practice to enhance productivity. In these sessions, you can visualize completing your tasks successfully, feeling a sense of accomplishment, and experiencing the rewards of your efforts. This form of mental rehearsal primes your brain for success, reinforcing positive feelings and motivating you to take action. Visualization can also be used to imagine yourself staying focused, calm, and productive throughout the day, which strengthens your ability to follow through on your goals.

Overall, building a meditation practice for productivity

is about creating a foundation of mental clarity, focus, and emotional balance that empowers you to stay on task and avoid procrastination. With regular practice, meditation not only helps reduce stress but also enhances your ability to concentrate, make better decisions, and approach challenges with a positive, productive mindset.

Training your focus

Training your focus involves intentionally working to enhance your ability to concentrate for extended periods while minimizing distractions. It's a skill that can be developed over time with practice, consistency, and the right techniques. Focus is not something that simply comes naturally to everyone; it's a muscle that needs to be exercised and strengthened, much like physical fitness. At its core, training your focus is about building habits that promote sustained attention and reducing mental fatigue.

One effective way to train your focus is to set specific goals and work on tasks that require full engagement. When you're clear on what you need to do and can fully immerse yourself in the task, you naturally enhance your ability to concentrate. Creating an environment that supports this focus is also crucial. A space free from distractions, like noise or clutter, helps your brain tune into the task rather than scattering your attention. This environment allows you to stay present, gradually developing your ability to concentrate for longer periods.

Moreover, training your focus involves learning how to recognize when your attention is waning. Distractions are inevitable, and your mind will likely wander during focused work sessions. The key is not to get frustrated or judge yourself when this happens but instead to gently redirect your attention back to the task at hand. Practicing mindfulness can be an excellent way to strengthen this skill, as it encourages you to observe your thoughts without getting caught up in them. Each time you bring your attention back to your work, you're building your focus muscle, making it stronger over time.

Another important aspect of training your focus is being kind to yourself during the process. It's easy to get discouraged when you don't achieve the level of concentration you desire immediately. Focus requires both mental and emotional resilience, and the ability to bounce back from distractions or moments of lost concentration is part of the learning process. The more you practice staying present and redirecting your focus, the more your concentration will improve. Eventually, tasks that once seemed difficult to focus on will become easier, and your overall productivity will increase.

Finally, it's important to recognize that focus is not just about working harder; it's about working smarter. Training your focus involves balancing effort with rest. When you push yourself too hard without breaks, your ability to concentrate diminishes. Regular rest periods, whether through techniques like the Pomodoro method or simply taking a few minutes to stretch and recharge, help prevent mental exhaustion. By incorporating both focused work and mindful rest, you can create a rhythm that supports long-term concentration and enhances your productivity.

How to improve concentration through practice.

Improving concentration is a skill that requires consistent practice and the development of habits that support mental focus. Just as physical exercise strengthens muscles, mental exercises strengthen the brain's ability to concentrate. One of the most effective ways to improve concentration is by regularly engaging in focused activities that challenge your attention span, such as reading, puzzles, or even mindfulness practices like meditation. These activities train your brain to remain present, reducing distractions and increasing your ability to focus for longer periods.

Starting with small tasks that require your full attention can help you build concentration over time. It's important to gradually increase the duration of these tasks, as your ability to concentrate strengthens. In the beginning, your mind may wander frequently, but with continued effort, your ability to stay on task will improve. It's also essential to practice patience with yourself, understanding that improving concentration is a gradual process that requires time and consistent effort. The more you practice focusing, the more natural it becomes, allowing you to shift your attention away from distractions with ease.

One of the keys to improving concentration is understanding the role of mental energy. Just as your body gets fatigued from physical exertion, your mind can become tired from prolonged focus. Taking short breaks between focused tasks is critical for maintaining mental sharpness. By giving yourself permission to rest, even for just a few minutes, you're replenishing your mental energy and allowing your concentration to reset. Over time, this strategy will allow you to concentrate for longer stretches without feeling mentally drained.

Avoiding multitasking traps.

Multitasking may seem like an efficient way to get things done, but research shows that it actually impairs focus and reduces productivity. When you try to juggle multiple tasks at once, your brain is forced to switch between them, which creates cognitive overload and reduces the effectiveness of each task. The result is not only slower progress but also a higher likelihood of mistakes and errors. By focusing on one task at a time, you allow your brain to dedicate its full cognitive resources to that task, improving both speed and accuracy.

To avoid multitasking, it's important to recognize when it's happening and intentionally choose to focus on a single task. One way to do this is by setting clear goals for what you want to accomplish in a given period. When you know exactly what needs to be done, it's easier to resist the urge to check your phone or jump between tasks. Prioritizing tasks and creating a to-do list can also help keep you on track. When you commit to one task, you're more likely to finish it efficiently, leaving you with a sense of accomplishment that motivates you to move on to the next task.

Additionally, managing distractions is key to avoiding multitasking. If you have your phone or other devices nearby, it's easy to get sidetracked by notifications or messages. Creating a distraction-free environment, whether it's by turning off notifications or putting your phone in another room, allows you to stay focused on the task at hand. Setting boundaries with others can also be helpful in avoiding interruptions, particularly if you're working in a shared space. By making a conscious effort to limit distractions, you're eliminating the temptation to multitask, which ultimately enhances your productivity and focus.

Using focus-boosting exercises like the Pomodoro Technique.

The Pomodoro Technique is a popular time-management method that boosts focus and productivity by breaking work into short, focused intervals, typically lasting 25 minutes, followed by a short break. This technique helps train your brain to concentrate for shorter bursts, making it easier to stay focused without feeling overwhelmed. By working in these intervals, you're able to maintain mental sharpness and avoid the fatigue that can set in during longer periods of work. The breaks in between sessions allow you to recharge, ensuring that you remain productive throughout the day.

One of the benefits of the Pomodoro Technique is its simplicity. All you need is a timer to keep track of the work and break intervals. After completing four Pomodoros, you take a longer break, typically 15-30 minutes. This method helps create a rhythm of productivity and rest, keeping your energy levels balanced and preventing burnout. By using the Pomodoro Technique, you're training your brain to focus more effectively, making it easier to maintain concentration on tasks without feeling mentally fatigued.

Another key aspect of the Pomodoro Technique is the ability to track progress. As you complete each interval, you can visually see how much work you've accomplished, which can provide a sense of satisfaction and motivation. This structured approach reduces the temptation to procrastinate and helps you stay on task, knowing that you'll get a break after each focused interval. Additionally, if you find yourself getting distracted during a Pomodoro session, simply acknowledging the distraction and refocusing can help you build mental resilience over time.

Incorporating focus-boosting exercises like the Pomodoro Technique into your routine is an effective way to train your brain to concentrate and stay on task. By regularly practicing these techniques, you'll improve your ability to maintain focus, avoid multitasking traps, and boost your overall productivity.

7

MASTERING SELF-DISCIPLINE

What self-discipline really is

Self-discipline is often misunderstood as simply a matter of willpower. Many people believe that some individuals are naturally born with a higher level of self-discipline, while others struggle with it. This perception creates a false divide between those who seem to succeed effortlessly and those who feel like they're always battling their impulses. In reality, self-discipline is much more than a single act of willpower; it's a collection of habits, decisions, and behaviors that can be learned, strengthened, and refined over time. The idea that self-discipline is innate, something you're either born with or not, is a myth that prevents many from even attempting to build it in the first place.

Dispelling the myth of willpower.

Dispelling the myth of willpower is crucial in understanding that self-discipline is not about having an unshakeable inner strength that allows some people to succeed while others falter. Willpower is often romanticized as a magical force that people tap into when they need to push themselves through tough situations. The problem with this myth is that it suggests willpower is a finite resource—something you either have or don't have. It implies that success in overcoming procrastination or achieving goals is merely about summoning the strength to push through discomfort, with little regard for strategy or consistency.

The truth is, willpower alone is rarely enough to produce lasting change. It can be a helpful initial motivator in certain situations, but it is not sustainable over the long term. When people rely solely on willpower, they often burn out or fall back into old habits. This is because willpower is not something you can consistently depend on; it's a fragile resource that can get depleted with repeated use. In stressful or demanding moments, people may feel like they've exhausted their willpower and find it difficult to continue pushing forward. What often happens is that they resort to easier, more comfortable choices—like procrastinating or giving in to distractions—because the mental energy to stay disciplined has been used up.

To truly overcome procrastination and build self-discipline, it's essential to shift away from the reliance on willpower and focus instead on creating systems and habits that support productivity and consistency. Instead of thinking of self-discipline as an act of sheer willpower, it's more effective to think of it as a series of small, deliberate actions taken over time. These actions become ingrained as habits, reducing the mental energy needed to make decisions. The more consistent you are with your efforts, the less you have to rely on willpower, because discipline becomes part of your routine. Additionally, focusing on creating environments that remove distractions or make tasks easier to accomplish can lessen the need for willpower altogether. By setting up your life in a way that supports your goals, you can effectively bypass the constant need for willpower and instead rely on automatic actions that drive success.

The connection between discipline and freedom.

The connection between discipline and freedom is often misunderstood, as many people see discipline as a restrictive force, limiting their choices and suppressing their desires. However, the truth is that discipline, far from being a form of control, is a pathway to greater freedom. The key to understanding this connection lies in recognizing that true freedom is not about having unlimited options or doing whatever we want without consequence; it's about having the ability to make choices that align with our long-term values and goals. Discipline gives us the structure and self-control necessary to prioritize what truly matters, freeing us from the anxiety and chaos that comes from constantly reacting to distractions and impulsive decisions.

When we lack discipline, we find ourselves constantly reacting to short-term temptations and external pressures, which often leads to regret and dissatisfaction. We might procrastinate, give in to distractions, or put off important tasks, which creates a cycle of stress and missed opportunities. In contrast, when we cultivate discipline, we can take control of our time, energy, and focus. This control allows us to break free from the tyranny of distractions and the constant pull of immediate gratification. With discipline, we're able to make deliberate choices that reflect our deeper goals, which ultimately gives us more freedom to pursue what we truly want, whether it's personal growth, financial security, or meaningful relationships.

Discipline also frees us from the need to constantly make decisions or exert effort in every moment. When we develop disciplined habits, we create a system where many of our choices are made in advance, reducing the mental load and decision fatigue that can be overwhelming. For example, setting aside specific times for exercise, work, or leisure eliminates the need to repeatedly decide when or how to fit them into our day. This creates a sense of mental clarity and purpose, which allows us to focus on what truly matters, free from the constant worry about our responsibilities. Essentially, discipline provides a framework within which we can experience more freedom, because it gives us the tools to make progress toward our desired outcomes without being constantly derailed by distractions or lack of direction. In this way, self-discipline becomes a means of achieving personal freedom, empowering us to live a more intentional, fulfilling life.

Why self-discipline is a skill, not a trait.

Self-discipline is often misunderstood as an inherent trait that some people are simply born with, while others are not. This misconception can be discouraging for those who struggle with procrastination or find it hard to stay focused. The truth, however, is that self-discipline is a skill that can be developed over time with consistent effort, just like any other ability. While some individuals may appear to have a natural inclination toward discipline, it is likely the result of habits, strategies, and environmental factors that they have cultivated, rather than an innate trait they possess.

When we view self-discipline as a skill, we recognize that it is something that can be learned, practiced, and refined. Skills are developed through repetition and experience, not through some mysterious, unchangeable characteristic. Just like learning to play an instrument or mastering a sport, self-discipline requires practice and patience. It's not about relying on some burst of willpower in the moment, but about consistently making decisions that align with our long-term goals and values. Over time, these small acts of self-control compound, creating a habit loop that reinforces disciplined behavior and ultimately leads to greater success in achieving our objectives.

Seeing self-discipline as a skill also removes the pressure of thinking that we either have it or we don't. Instead of feeling defeated or hopeless when we fall short of our goals, we can approach our lapses with a mindset of improvement. Every setback becomes an opportunity to learn and adjust, not a sign of personal failure. By focusing on developing the skill of self-discipline, we allow ourselves the freedom to grow, experiment, and evolve. Through this perspective, we understand that discipline isn't about being perfect or having an unbreakable will—it's about refining a skill over time, adjusting our approach as needed, and continuing to move forward with intention and persistence. The more we practice and reinforce these behaviors, the more self-discipline becomes a natural part of our lives, leading to lasting personal transformation.

Strengthening your willpower

Strengthening your willpower involves developing the ability to resist immediate temptations in favor of long-term goals, and it is a skill that can be nurtured with practice. One of the most effective techniques for resisting temptation is learning to create physical or mental distance from it. For instance, when faced with a temptation to procrastinate, you can remove distractions or change your environment to reduce the chance of giving in. Another powerful technique is to practice mindfulness, which allows you to become aware of the impulse before acting on it. By recognizing the urge to give in as just a passing thought or feeling, you can acknowledge it without succumbing to it. Additionally, having a clear sense of why you are resisting the temptation—whether it's the bigger goal you are working toward or the negative consequences of yielding—can help you stay focused and committed in the moment. It's also important to build in "mental breaks" to allow yourself rest and recovery, ensuring that your willpower doesn't feel drained over time. Strengthening willpower is not about being perfect at resisting temptation, but about developing strategies to manage impulses effectively.

Techniques to resist temptation.

Resisting temptation is a vital skill for overcoming procrastination and achieving long-term success. Techniques to resist temptation are not just about sheer willpower, but about creating a strategy to minimize the impact of tempting distractions. One of the most effective techniques is called "delay and distract." This involves allowing yourself to feel the impulse to give in but delaying it by a few minutes. During that time, you distract yourself with another task or focus on something unrelated to the temptation. Often, the urge will pass as the mind moves on to other thoughts.

Another technique is called "temptation bundling." This involves pairing something enjoyable with a task you want to avoid. For example, you could allow yourself to watch your favorite show or listen to a podcast only while you're doing something productive, like cleaning or working on a project. By associating enjoyable experiences with productive behavior, the brain starts to rewire its response, making it easier to stay on task. Another valuable tool is "environment design," which involves modifying your physical or digital surroundings to remove temptations. This could be as simple as turning off notifications on your phone or setting up a quiet workspace that minimizes distractions. The idea is to change your environment in a way that reduces your exposure to things that might derail your focus. Additionally, mindfulness can help you stay grounded and aware of your impulses. By practicing mindfulness techniques, such as focusing on your breath, you can gain the space to make conscious choices instead of reacting impulsively.

Lastly, commitment devices can be a powerful tool in resisting temptation. This involves making a public commitment or placing constraints on your behavior in advance. For example, you could tell a friend about a goal you are working toward or set up a system where you pay a penalty if you fail to follow through. These external commitments can provide added motivation to resist temptation, as the consequences of giving in become more tangible. Ultimately, resisting temptation is about making conscious decisions, altering your environment, and establishing support systems that hold you accountable. Through practice, these techniques can significantly improve your ability to stay focused and achieve your goals, even in the face of distractions.

How to recover from lapses in discipline.

Recovering from lapses in discipline is an essential part of building long-term success, as perfection is not the goal—progress is. Everyone faces moments when they lose focus or fall off track, and how you respond to these lapses can significantly influence your future success. The key to recovery is to approach the situation with self-compassion rather than self-criticism. Guilt and shame can fuel further procrastination and diminish your motivation, whereas a more compassionate response allows you to bounce back more effectively. Acknowledge the lapse without judgment, understand why it happened, and remind yourself that setbacks are part of the learning process.

One effective strategy for recovering from lapses is to focus on the next step instead of dwelling on what went wrong. When you find yourself off track, instead of letting the setback spiral into a larger issue, break down the next action you can take into something simple and achievable. This prevents feelings of overwhelm and helps you regain momentum quickly. It's also important to practice reflection—take a moment to identify the underlying causes of the lapse. Was it an external distraction, a lack of motivation, or perhaps a deeper issue such as fatigue or burnout? Understanding the root cause can help you put systems in place to prevent future lapses and stay more disciplined moving forward.

Another powerful tool is to re-establish your commitment by revisiting your goals and reminding yourself why you started in the first place. When you reconnect with your long-term purpose, it reignites your motivation and drives you to keep going. Also, focusing on the positive progress you've made, no matter how small, can help you shift your mindset. It's easy to focus on perceived failures, but acknowledging the successes—even minor ones—creates a foundation of resilience. Instead of letting a lapse define your trajectory, use it as a learning opportunity to enhance your self-discipline in the future.

Sometimes, re-establishing discipline requires re-evaluating your routines and adjusting them as needed. If you find that lapses in discipline happen frequently in certain situations, it might be a sign that your current habits or strategies are not working. Experiment with new approaches and systems to regain control, whether that's setting clearer boundaries, adjusting your schedule, or seeking additional support. By embracing flexibility and continually refining your approach, you'll increase your ability to recover quickly from lapses and ultimately strengthen your self-discipline over time.

Building long-term resilience.

Recovering from lapses in discipline is an essential part of building long-term success, as perfection is not the goal—progress is. Everyone faces moments when they lose focus or fall off track, and how you respond to these lapses can significantly influence your future success. The key to recovery is to approach the situation with self-compassion rather than self-criticism. Guilt and shame can fuel further procrastination and diminish your motivation, whereas a more compassionate response allows you to bounce back more effectively. Acknowledge the lapse without judgment, understand why it happened, and remind yourself that setbacks are part of the learning process.

One effective strategy for recovering from lapses is to focus on the next step instead of dwelling on what went wrong. When you find yourself off track, instead of letting the setback spiral into a larger issue, break down the next action you can take into something simple and achievable. This prevents feelings of overwhelm and helps you regain momentum quickly. It's also important to practice reflection—take a moment to identify the underlying causes of the lapse. Was it an external distraction, a lack of motivation, or perhaps a deeper issue such as fatigue or burnout? Understanding the root cause can help you put systems in place to prevent future lapses and stay more disciplined moving forward.

Another powerful tool is to re-establish your commitment by revisiting your goals and reminding yourself why you started in the first place. When you reconnect with your long-term purpose, it reignites your motivation and drives you to keep going. Also, focusing on the positive progress you've made, no matter how small, can help you shift your mindset. It's easy to focus on perceived failures, but acknowledging the successes—even minor ones—creates a foundation of resilience. Instead of letting a lapse define your trajectory, use it as a learning opportunity to enhance your self-discipline in the future.

Cultivating accountability

Using accountability partners effectively is a powerful way to cultivate discipline and overcome procrastination. An accountability partner is someone who checks in on your progress, offers encouragement, and helps you stay focused on your goals. The key to using an accountability partner effectively is establishing clear, mutual expectations. It's important that both individuals have defined roles, with specific goals, deadlines, and regular check-ins. This creates a sense of responsibility not just to yourself, but also to someone else, which can significantly enhance motivation. The relationship should be built on trust, openness, and constructive feedback, ensuring that both partners feel empowered to hold each other accountable without judgment. Moreover, accountability works best when the partner is supportive yet firm, offering praise for progress while gently reminding you of your commitments when you fall off track.

Using accountability partners effectively.

Using accountability partners effectively involves more than just telling someone about your goals. It's about creating a relationship where both individuals are committed to supporting each other's progress, offering constructive feedback, and maintaining consistent communication. The first step in using an accountability partner effectively is to establish clear expectations. Both parties should understand the specific goals that need to be achieved, the timeline for accomplishing them, and the frequency of check-ins. Without these clear parameters, the relationship could lose focus and become less effective.

An effective accountability partnership relies on mutual respect and open communication. It's essential to set up a safe environment where both individuals feel comfortable sharing their progress, challenges, and even failures. If the partner feels like they will be judged or criticized harshly, they may be less likely to open up and seek support when needed. Accountability partners should also be reliable—someone who can commit to the process of checking in regularly and providing feedback.

The structure of your check-ins also matters. They should be regular enough to create a sense of urgency, but flexible enough to accommodate life's unpredictable nature. For example, weekly meetings might be ideal for some, while others may benefit from bi-weekly check-ins. These check-ins can take various forms: in-person meetings, phone calls, or virtual sessions. During these check-ins, the accountability partner should focus on the process, not just the outcome. This helps keep the focus on the effort and improvement rather than just ticking off completed tasks. By discussing obstacles, celebrating small wins, and reevaluating strategies, the partner helps maintain momentum and adjusts tactics when necessary.

Accountability partners can also serve as a source of motivation and encouragement. Sometimes, just knowing that someone else is aware of your goals can propel you to act. Their support can provide emotional reinforcement when motivation wanes, and they can remind you of your capabilities when doubt sets in. However, this relationship should also be balanced; the accountability partner's role isn't to do the work for you, but rather to offer guidance and keep you on track. Effective accountability requires both partners to hold each other to their commitments while fostering a sense of empathy, understanding, and encouragement.

How public commitments can motivate action.

Public commitments can significantly increase motivation and encourage action because they introduce an element of social accountability. When you make a commitment in front of others, you create a sense of responsibility not only to yourself but also to those who are aware of your goal. The idea of social pressure—whether positive or negative—can push you to follow through with your promises to avoid the embarrassment or guilt of failing to meet your publicly stated goals.

One of the psychological factors at play is the fear of judgment or social disapproval. Humans are inherently social creatures, and the desire to be seen as reliable and competent in the eyes of others can drive us to take action. Making your commitment public adds a layer of external expectation. For instance, telling a group of friends that you're going to complete a certain project by a specific deadline increases the likelihood that you'll work harder to meet that goal. You may fear letting down the people who are expecting you to deliver, and that fear can act as a motivator.

Public commitments also create a sense of urgency. The moment a goal is shared with others, the timeline for achieving that goal becomes more tangible. There's a real-world consequence to not following through, and this can spur action. People may even feel a greater sense of pride in achieving their goals if they have made those goals known to others, as success is not only personal but also publicly acknowledged. This external recognition can serve as an incentive to keep working towards the goal, especially when the commitment is tied to a specific outcome that others will notice.

Additionally, public commitments can help create a support network. When you publicly state your intentions, others can offer encouragement, check in on your progress, and even help hold you accountable. This network of support makes it harder to back out of your commitment because you're not alone in the process. The social bond formed by the shared knowledge of your goal can keep you engaged, provide emotional reinforcement, and even bring in external resources or advice that you might not have accessed otherwise.

In some cases, the public nature of the commitment can create an intrinsic desire to "save face" or maintain one's reputation. This becomes a powerful motivator to continue working toward the goal, even when challenges arise. Whether it's for the sake of pride, self-respect, or avoiding social disapproval, the act of making a public commitment often provides the external pressure and encouragement necessary to spur action and prevent procrastination.

Creating self-monitoring systems.

Creating self-monitoring systems is an effective strategy for increasing productivity, managing goals, and overcoming procrastination. Self-monitoring involves actively tracking your progress toward achieving your goals, assessing your behaviors, and holding yourself accountable. By incorporating regular checks and evaluations into your routine, you can gain insight into where you might be falling short, identify areas for improvement, and stay motivated as you observe your incremental progress.

One of the key elements of self-monitoring is establishing measurable goals and defining what success looks like. It's essential to break down larger goals into smaller, manageable tasks that can be tracked on a daily or weekly basis. For example, if you're working on a writing project, you might set a goal to write 500 words a day. Tracking this progress can be as simple as marking off a daily checklist or logging your word count in a spreadsheet. This approach helps make progress tangible and reinforces a sense of accomplishment as you see the work accumulating.

To make the most of self-monitoring, it's important to choose tools that fit your personality and preferences. This could range from using a digital app or spreadsheet to keep track of tasks and deadlines, to employing more traditional methods such as a physical planner or journal. The key is consistency and the ability to review your progress regularly.

Some individuals might find it helpful to use visual representations of progress, such as charts or graphs, to see their improvements over time. For others, simply checking off completed tasks might be enough to feel a sense of achievement and maintain focus.

Another benefit of self-monitoring is that it provides an opportunity for self-reflection. As you track your actions, you can also assess your patterns of behavior. Are there times when you're more productive? Do certain distractions or negative habits emerge frequently? Self-monitoring allows you to recognize these patterns and make adjustments as needed. For instance, if you notice that you consistently procrastinate during a particular time of day, you can experiment with shifting your work schedule or addressing the underlying issues contributing to the delay.

Regular reviews also provide an opportunity to adjust your goals and strategies. If you're not making as much progress as you'd like, the data you collect from self-monitoring can help you pinpoint the reasons behind it—whether it's overambitious goals, inadequate resources, or a lack of clear priorities. With this information, you can make better decisions about how to proceed, adjusting your approach rather than staying stuck in a pattern of unproductive behavior.

The act of self-monitoring also fosters a sense of accountability. When you are actively tracking your progress, you are more likely to stay committed to your tasks because you have a constant reminder of what you've done and what remains to be done. This can help prevent distractions and procrastination by keeping you aligned with your objectives and focused on what needs attention.

Ultimately, creating a self-monitoring system empowers you

to take control of your actions, make necessary adjustments in real time, and track the cumulative effects of your efforts. By making this process a routine part of your life, you can maintain focus, minimize procrastination, and enhance your overall productivity.

8

PRACTICAL TOOLS FOR OVERCOMING PROCRASTINATION

Leveraging productivity apps and tools

Leveraging productivity apps and tools can significantly enhance your ability to stay organized, meet deadlines, and combat procrastination. With the right tools, you can streamline your tasks, maintain focus, and ensure that nothing slips through the cracks. The key to using these tools effectively lies in selecting the right ones for your specific needs and consistently applying them to stay on track. Ultimately, leveraging the right productivity apps and tools can help you stay organized, maintain momentum, and collaborate seamlessly with others. Whether you're managing tasks individually, setting reminders to stay on track, or working with a team, these tools can help you maximize your efficiency and overcome procrastination. The key is to integrate them into your daily routine and use them consistently to streamline your workflow and achieve your goals.

Best apps for task management.

When it comes to task management, choosing the right apps can make a significant difference in how efficiently and effectively you organize your day. The best apps for task management are designed to streamline your workflow, improve organization, and keep you focused on completing tasks. There are various apps available, each catering to different preferences and work styles, so it's essential to understand what each offers to select the one that best fits your needs.

Trello is one of the most popular task management tools, known for its visually appealing and intuitive kanban-style boards. It allows you to create boards for different projects and add cards for individual tasks. You can organize tasks by stages, such as "To Do," "In Progress," and "Completed," making it easy to track the status of each task. Trello also offers collaboration features, so you can assign tasks to team members, set deadlines, and attach files or links. The flexibility of Trello makes it perfect for both personal use and collaborative team projects. With its drag-and-drop interface and simple layout, Trello is ideal for people who prefer a clear visual representation of their tasks.

Todoist is another highly regarded task management app, known for its simplicity and powerful features. It allows users to create tasks, set deadlines, and prioritize work with ease. One standout feature of Todoist is its natural language processing, which lets you quickly add tasks with specific dates, like "Buy groceries tomorrow." You can organize tasks into projects and assign priority levels, making it easier to focus on what's most important. Todoist also offers reminders and integrates with other tools, such as Google Calendar, so you never miss a deadline. Whether you're managing simple to-do lists or more complex projects, Todoist is a versatile tool that's easy to use and very effective for personal productivity.

Asana is another excellent task management app, especially for people working on teams or managing complex projects. It offers features like task assignments, due dates, dependencies, and project timelines. Asana's ability to break projects into smaller tasks and track progress over time helps ensure that projects stay on track. You can organize tasks into projects, assign them to specific team members, and even track overall project progress through its timeline and reporting features. Asana also offers collaboration tools, like comments and file attachments, so team members can communicate within the app and stay aligned on goals. For people who need more advanced project management tools, Asana is an ideal choice because of its robust functionality and flexible options.

Microsoft To Do is another solid option for task management, particularly for those who use Microsoft Office products. It allows you to create simple to-do lists, set due dates, and organize tasks by category. You can also add steps to tasks, making it easy to break down larger projects into smaller actions. What sets Microsoft To Do apart is its seamless integration with other Microsoft Office apps, such as Outlook, making it especially helpful for people already using the Office ecosystem. For those who need a straightforward task manager that syncs across all their devices, Microsoft To Do is a great option.

Finally, ClickUp is a powerful all-in-one project management tool that helps you manage tasks, documents, goals, and timelines. Its customizable interface allows you to adapt it to your specific needs, whether you're managing a personal to-do list or coordinating an entire team's workflow. ClickUp offers features like task hierarchies, goal tracking, and time management tools, making it suitable for both small teams and large enterprises. The app's flexibility allows you to manage projects with a high degree of detail, ensuring you stay on top of every aspect of your work.

Each of these task management apps offers unique features that can help streamline your workflow, whether you're managing personal tasks or working as part of a team. The best app for you will depend on your individual preferences, work style, and the level of complexity you need in your task management system. By experimenting with different options, you can find the tool that best helps you stay organized and focused, ultimately reducing procrastination and boosting productivity.

How to use reminders effectively.

Using reminders effectively can be a game-changer in managing tasks and staying on track with deadlines. Reminders are simple yet powerful tools that help you stay focused, organized, and reduce the chances of forgetting important tasks. To make the most out of reminders, it's important to know when to set them, how to customize them, and the best ways to integrate them into your daily routine.

One of the first steps to using reminders effectively is determining what tasks actually need a reminder. Not everything requires a prompt, so it's crucial to prioritize tasks that are either time-sensitive, have multiple steps, or tend to be easily overlooked. For example, setting a reminder for a meeting, an upcoming deadline, or an appointment is useful, while setting a reminder for routine tasks that don't require immediate attention might be unnecessary. By focusing on key tasks, you can prevent overwhelm from an excess of reminders and keep them meaningful and effective.

Customizing reminders is another key aspect of using them well. Many reminder apps allow you to set reminders with different levels of urgency and frequency. For instance, you can set a reminder for a task in the morning to give you time to prepare, and another one an hour before the task is due. Adjusting the timing and frequency of reminders based on how much time you need to complete a task can prevent procrastination and ensure you're well-prepared. For longer-term projects, setting recurring reminders can help you break them into smaller, manageable chunks, giving you a continuous sense of progress.

To prevent reminders from becoming background noise and losing their effectiveness, it's important to make them as specific as possible. Vague reminders like "work on report" may not be as useful as more detailed prompts, such as "finish introduction of report by 3 p.m." When you create reminders with clear objectives and deadlines, they become more actionable, which increases the likelihood of following through. Be specific about what you need to accomplish and by when, so your mind knows exactly what needs to be done when the reminder pops up.

Another important strategy is using multiple channels to ensure you don't miss a reminder. Most apps allow you to sync reminders across devices, whether it's your phone, computer, or smart watch. This way, you'll get notified through different platforms, whether you're at your desk or on the go. You can also integrate your reminders into your calendar or task management apps for seamless tracking of deadlines and appointments. A synchronized system helps you stay on top of your tasks without relying on a single reminder source.

While reminders are useful, it's essential to maintain focus and avoid becoming overly reliant on them. If you find yourself constantly checking reminders or feeling overwhelmed by them, you might need to reassess how many reminders you're setting or how much time you're leaving between tasks. There's a fine line between helpful nudges and excessive notifications that disrupt your focus, so it's important to balance reminders with periods of uninterrupted work.

Finally, using reminders to build positive habits is another effective technique. For instance, setting daily reminders to review your goals or plan your day can help you build a routine. As you regularly respond to these reminders, the tasks may eventually become ingrained in your schedule, reducing the need for constant nudges. Similarly, by associating reminders with healthy habits like exercising or taking breaks, you can increase productivity and well-being over time.

In short, reminders are a powerful tool to help you stay organized, focused, and on track. When used effectively, they can prevent procrastination, reduce mental clutter, and help you stay aligned with your goals. By choosing the right tasks to remind yourself about, customizing your reminders for clarity and urgency, and ensuring they're synchronized across your devices, you'll find yourself managing your time and workload more efficiently. However, it's also important to strike a balance and avoid overloading yourself with too many reminders, so they remain effective in supporting your productivity.

Tools for collaboration and delegation.

When it comes to collaboration and delegation, the right tools can make a significant difference in how effectively teams work together and how tasks are managed. These tools allow individuals to delegate responsibilities, track progress, share information, and ensure that everyone is aligned with their goals, resulting in a more organized and efficient workflow. Let's explore how these tools work and how they can be used to improve collaboration and delegation.

Collaboration tools provide a centralized platform where team members can communicate, share files, and coordinate efforts, even if they're working remotely. Platforms like Slack, Microsoft Teams, or Google Workspace enable real-time communication, whether it's through chat, voice calls, or video conferences. These tools eliminate the need for scattered communication across emails, text messages, and other platforms, making it easier to keep track of discussions, decisions, and tasks. You can create channels or groups specific to projects or topics, ensuring that only relevant conversations are taking place in each space. This helps reduce the noise and increases the clarity of communication.

Delegation tools, on the other hand, allow managers or team leaders to assign tasks clearly and efficiently. Project management platforms like Asana, Trello, and Monday.com are excellent for this purpose. They let you break down large projects into smaller, actionable tasks that can be assigned to individuals with specific deadlines. These tools offer visibility into who is responsible for what, and they allow team members to see the status of their tasks in real time. When delegating tasks, you can ensure that every person knows their responsibilities, and you can easily track the progress of each task to ensure everything is on schedule.

The key to successful delegation is making sure that tasks are assigned based on the strengths, skills, and availability of the team members. Tools like Trello or Asana often include options for priority settings, so you can designate what needs to be done immediately versus what can be tackled later. When using these platforms, it's helpful to include clear instructions, deadlines, and any necessary context to ensure that everyone understands their role and expectations.

In addition to delegation, collaboration tools also enable seamless sharing of resources. Tools like Google Drive, Dropbox, and Microsoft OneDrive allow team members to share documents, files, and data easily. These platforms also support real-time editing, meaning that multiple people can work on the same document simultaneously. This eliminates the need for back-and-forth email exchanges and reduces version control issues, making collaboration more streamlined and efficient. With everything stored in a central location, team members can access the most up-to-date files without confusion, ensuring everyone is working with the correct information.

Another important feature of collaboration tools is task tracking. Platforms like Asana, ClickUp, and Teamwork provide visual representations of task progress through boards, calendars, and timelines. These tools enable team members to see who's doing what, track due dates, and quickly identify any roadblocks or bottlenecks. They also help keep everyone accountable by making the progress of each task transparent. With these tools, everyone on the team can quickly assess the status of various assignments and take necessary action if a deadline is approaching or if a task is delayed.

For delegating tasks remotely, tools that offer time tracking can be especially helpful. Tools like Toggl or Harvest allow team members to track the amount of time spent on tasks, providing insight into how efficiently work is being done. This can be particularly beneficial for managing freelancers, contractors, or remote teams, as it ensures that everyone's time is being used effectively. Additionally, having clear time tracking enables managers to allocate resources more efficiently and make adjustments to workloads if necessary.

Lastly, feedback and reporting tools are essential for maintaining clarity and improving collaboration. Many project management and collaboration platforms offer options for providing feedback on tasks and projects. Team members can leave comments, tag each other in discussions, and provide suggestions, which helps to clarify expectations and improve results. Reporting features, such as Gantt charts or Kanban boards, give managers and team members a quick overview of task progress and deadlines, allowing them to make data-driven decisions.

In conclusion, collaboration and delegation tools are indispensable for streamlining workflows, enhancing communication, and ensuring the successful completion of tasks. By providing a platform for clear task assignment, transparent progress tracking, and effective communication, these tools improve both individual and team productivity. The key is to choose the right tools for your team's needs, be it for task management, file sharing, time tracking, or feedback, and integrate them seamlessly into your workflow. By doing so, you can eliminate inefficiencies, reduce misunderstandings, and create a collaborative environment where everyone can work together towards shared goals.

The power of checklists

Breaking tasks into steps is a powerful technique because it makes large, daunting tasks feel more manageable and less overwhelming. When you approach a project or assignment, it can often seem like an insurmountable challenge, especially if it's complex or unfamiliar. By breaking it down into smaller, more specific tasks, you give yourself clear, achievable goals that create a sense of progress as you complete each step. This approach also allows you to focus on one piece at a time, reducing the mental clutter of trying to think about everything at once. Instead of feeling anxious or procrastinating due to the perceived size of the project, you can focus on the smaller, more immediate actions that need to be taken. This incremental approach is effective because it keeps you from feeling paralyzed by the task, and it helps maintain momentum as you check off each step. Breaking tasks into smaller steps, designing actionable lists, and using visual progress trackers can significantly enhance productivity. These strategies make tasks feel more manageable, reduce procrastination, and provide clear markers of progress, ultimately helping you stay organized and motivated. By incorporating these techniques into your routine, you'll not only complete tasks more efficiently but also cultivate a sense of accomplishment that propels you toward your larger goals.

Why breaking tasks into steps works.

Breaking tasks into steps works because it makes large and complex tasks seem more approachable by turning them into manageable pieces. When we look at a big project or goal as a whole, it often feels overwhelming and can lead to procrastination. This happens because the sheer size or complexity of the task causes anxiety and mental blockages, making us feel like we don't know where to start or how to proceed. But when we break the task into smaller steps, the entire process becomes less intimidating, and we can begin with something simple and achievable.

Each step provides a clear, specific action, which gives us direction. We no longer have to worry about the entire task at once; instead, we focus only on the next small thing. This incremental approach not only reduces anxiety but also creates a sense of progress. Completing one step leads naturally to the next, and as we tick off each task, we build momentum and motivation. This helps us stay engaged and less likely to get distracted or overwhelmed.

Additionally, breaking tasks into smaller chunks helps with time management. When we split a large task into discrete steps, we can better estimate how long each one will take. This allows us to set realistic deadlines for each small part, making it easier to prioritize and stay on track. It also helps with managing energy levels. Instead of spending hours on something that feels like a huge burden, we can allocate specific, smaller time blocks to each step, reducing mental fatigue.

Moreover, breaking tasks into steps taps into the psychology of achievement. Every time we complete a step, our brain releases dopamine, the "feel-good" neurotransmitter. This positive reinforcement boosts our motivation and encourages us to continue progressing. As we check off each item, we get a sense of accomplishment, which drives us to keep going and ultimately finish the task.

In essence, breaking tasks into steps works because it simplifies the process, reduces anxiety, builds momentum, enhances time management, and taps into our brain's natural reward system. These benefits make it easier to start, stay focused, and keep going, ultimately making us more productive and less likely to procrastinate.

Designing actionable, clear to-do lists.

Designing actionable, clear to-do lists is essential for boosting productivity because it transforms vague tasks into specific actions that are easy to follow through on. The key is to make each item on the list precise and achievable. When tasks are too general or broad, like "work on project" or "clean the house," they don't offer enough clarity about what needs to be done. This lack of clarity can cause procrastination, as it's hard to get started on something that isn't well defined.

To design actionable to-do lists, each task should be broken down into clear, specific steps. For example, instead of "work on project," a more actionable task might be "outline project structure" or "write introduction paragraph." This gives the person a clear starting point and makes it easy to know exactly what to do next. The more specific the action, the easier it is to make progress.

Another important aspect of a clear to-do list is setting realistic and manageable goals. If you write down something too big or overwhelming, like "complete all assignments," it's more likely to be ignored. Instead, you could break it down into smaller, more achievable tasks such as "complete math assignment" or "draft English essay introduction." By focusing on smaller, bite-sized goals, each task feels less daunting and easier to tackle.

Additionally, prioritizing tasks is crucial for a functional to-do list. Not every task on the list will be equally urgent or important. Prioritizing allows you to focus on what needs to be done first, rather than wasting time on less important tasks. You can organize tasks by deadlines or by importance, ensuring that you tackle the most critical items first. This helps you feel in control and focused, reducing the likelihood of feeling overwhelmed by a long list of things to do.

Timeframes and deadlines can also make to-do lists more effective. By assigning a time limit to each task—like "spend 30 minutes on research" or "complete report draft by 3 PM"—you create a sense of urgency and a clear target for completion. This helps combat procrastination, as you have a defined endpoint for each task. Setting time limits also helps with time management, allowing you to gauge how long each task actually takes and adjust your schedule for future tasks accordingly.

Incorporating flexibility into your to-do list is another

important factor. Sometimes, things don't go as planned, and tasks may take longer than expected. A clear to-do list should leave room for adjustments. This flexibility reduces frustration when things go off track, making it easier to refocus and continue working without feeling defeated.

Lastly, checking off completed tasks is a powerful motivator. The act of crossing something off the list provides a sense of accomplishment, which reinforces positive behavior and encourages you to keep going. This visual progress can be incredibly motivating and satisfying, and it serves as a reminder of how much you've already accomplished, even if the list still looks long.

In conclusion, designing actionable, clear to-do lists is about breaking down tasks into specific, manageable steps, prioritizing what needs to be done first, setting realistic timeframes, and leaving room for flexibility. This approach turns a seemingly overwhelming task into a series of small, achievable actions, making it easier to stay focused, organized, and productive.

Using visual progress trackers.

Using visual progress trackers is a highly effective strategy for maintaining motivation, focus, and a sense of accomplishment as you work through tasks. These trackers provide a tangible representation of the progress you've made and create a visual reminder of the work still to be done, which can help keep you engaged and on track.

Visual progress trackers come in various forms, from simple checklists to more elaborate graphs and charts, depending on the type of work and your preferences. One of the most common and simple types is a progress bar. A progress bar gives you a clear, visual representation of how far you've come and how much is left to do. It's motivating because you can see your progress in real time, and as the bar fills up, it provides a sense of completion and forward movement. The act of watching the bar fill up can give you the positive reinforcement needed to keep pushing through, especially on larger tasks that may seem overwhelming when viewed in their entirety.

Another type of visual progress tracker is a color-coded or numbered checklist. When you break down larger tasks into smaller, more specific actions, you can assign each task a number or color to indicate its level of priority, status, or completion. The sense of accomplishment that comes from crossing off each item, especially when you see the list shrinking, can build momentum and help combat procrastination. It also allows you to visually assess which tasks remain and which have been completed, providing a clear overview of what needs to be done.

For those working on long-term goals, progress trackers can take the form of calendars or goal-setting charts that span weeks or months. These can include monthly planners with spaces to mark off when certain milestones or tasks are completed, or larger charts with boxes to check off over time. Such trackers offer a broader view of your progress, which can be particularly useful for bigger projects or long-term habits. This visual overview not only gives you a sense of how much you've accomplished but also provides motivation to keep going, as you begin to see more boxes checked and milestones met.

In addition to these, there are digital tools that allow for visual progress tracking, including apps that help you break down tasks and visually represent your progress. Apps like Trello, Asana, or even Google Keep allow users to set up boards, lists, and task cards that can be visually organized and moved around. These digital trackers often come with additional features, such as deadlines, reminders, and the ability to track subtasks, which can make it easier to stay organized and ensure that nothing falls through the cracks.

The psychological benefits of using visual progress trackers are significant. Humans are inherently motivated by visual feedback. Seeing tangible evidence of your progress provides a sense of accomplishment, reinforcing the behavior and encouraging you to continue. This is particularly true when working on long-term projects or goals, where progress may feel slow or invisible if you don't have a clear way to track it. By creating a visual representation of your work, you make progress more concrete and satisfying, which helps overcome feelings of stagnation or overwhelm.

Moreover, visual progress trackers help manage expectations by making the process more transparent. It allows you to realistically assess how much you've done and how much is left, which helps prevent feelings of frustration or self-doubt. It also creates a sense of accountability, as you have a clear visual record of your progress that you can refer back to.

In summary, using visual progress trackers helps keep you motivated by providing clear, tangible representations of your progress. Whether through simple checklists, color-coded systems, or digital tools, these trackers create positive reinforcement, help you manage long-term goals, and offer an effective way to stay focused and organized. By seeing your progress visually, you turn the abstract concept of "progress" into something concrete, which makes it easier to continue pushing toward your goals.

Customizing your environment

Creating a workspace that promotes focus is essential for overcoming procrastination and boosting productivity. The environment you work in has a profound effect on your mental state, energy levels, and ability to concentrate. A cluttered, noisy, or disorganized workspace can distract you, making it more difficult to focus on the task at hand. To foster focus, it's important to create an environment that is both functional and conducive to deep work. This can involve organizing your workspace so that everything you need is within easy reach and minimizing distractions. For example, consider investing in a comfortable chair, a clean desk, and proper lighting that reduces strain on your eyes. Reducing clutter not only gives you a sense of order but can also have a calming effect on your mind, helping you to stay on track and focused.

By customizing your environment to suit your needs, you set yourself up for success. A carefully curated workspace, a reliable work ritual, and control over environmental distractions all work together to enhance focus and productivity. These strategies help you transition smoothly into work mode, reduce procrastination triggers, and keep you on task, creating an environment that supports your goals and fosters consistent progress.

Creating a workspace that promotes focus.

Creating a workspace that promotes focus requires intentional design choices that foster concentration, minimize distractions, and set a clear boundary between work and relaxation. Your environment greatly influences your mental state, and by optimizing it, you can significantly enhance your ability to focus and engage in tasks with greater efficiency.

First, you need to consider the physical layout of the space. The less clutter there is around you, the easier it will be to concentrate. A messy environment can cause your mind to feel similarly scattered, leading to procrastination or difficulty in completing tasks. To promote focus, keep only the essential items on your desk or work area. This includes materials related directly to the task at hand, such as your computer, documents, or a notebook. Organizing your workspace into zones, with specific areas for different activities, can also help create a mental separation between tasks and prevent them from blending together.

Ergonomics plays a key role in creating a focus-friendly workspace. If your chair is uncomfortable or your desk is too high or low, you'll constantly shift around in search of comfort, breaking your concentration. A comfortable chair that supports your back, an adjustable desk that suits your height, and a monitor at eye level will allow you to focus for longer periods without physical discomfort. This helps to keep your energy and focus levels up, without constant interruptions from aches or discomfort.

Another important factor is lighting. Lighting has a profound effect on your ability to focus. Natural light is ideal, as it mimics the rhythm of our circadian cycle and can positively impact mood and productivity. If natural light isn't available, it's important to choose light sources that are bright but not too harsh. Overhead fluorescent lights can often cause eye strain, while dim lighting can induce tiredness or make you feel sluggish. A desk lamp with adjustable brightness is a great way to provide focused lighting without over-stimulating the senses.

Sound is another element to consider when creating a workspace that promotes focus. Noise distractions can significantly impact concentration. For some, complete silence works best, while others may need background noise. If you find yourself distracted by sounds from outside your space, noise-canceling headphones or playing ambient noise such as white noise or instrumental music can help. Alternatively, using soundproofing methods, such as adding carpets, curtains, or wall panels, can minimize disruptive sounds from entering your workspace.

Personalizing your workspace in a way that fosters positivity and motivation is also crucial. While you want to avoid unnecessary clutter, having a few personal touches, like motivational quotes, artwork, or a plant, can create a sense of comfort and inspiration. A positive, aesthetically pleasing environment can help you feel more engaged with your work, which increases focus. However, it's important to strike a balance so that these personal items don't turn into distractions themselves.

Lastly, setting clear boundaries for your workspace is essential. When possible, dedicate a specific area solely for work, and avoid mixing this space with areas for leisure or relaxation. By creating a space that is exclusively for productivity, you condition your mind to enter a focused state whenever you are in that environment.

In essence, a workspace that promotes focus is one that minimizes distractions, supports your physical comfort, and enhances your mental state for productivity. By being mindful of the layout, ergonomics, lighting, sound, and personalization, you can create an environment that keeps you focused and energized throughout your workday.

Setting up rituals to transition into work mode.

Setting up rituals to transition into work mode is about creating a routine or series of actions that signal to your brain that it's time to focus and be productive. Just as you might have a ritual before bed to signal that it's time to wind down, having a structured pre-work ritual helps establish a mental separation between leisure or other activities and work. This transition can make it easier to switch gears, prepare mentally, and get into a focused mindset more quickly.

One of the first aspects of setting up a work ritual is identifying a consistent cue or action that serves as a trigger to start the day. This can be as simple as making a cup of coffee, stretching, or organizing your desk. The key is consistency. By performing the same sequence of actions before you begin working, you begin to associate that ritual with the state of focus required for productive work. For example, setting aside a few minutes to tidy up your workspace, turning on your computer, or checking your task list can mentally prepare you to dive into the work ahead. Repeating this process every day conditions your brain to recognize that work is starting, which helps to eliminate the confusion that can arise when you try to dive straight into a task without preparation.

Rituals can also include sensory elements that signal the beginning of work. Lighting a specific candle or playing certain types of music as you start your work can create a calm environment that promotes focus. These sensory cues can help trigger your brain's state of readiness for work, creating a mental association between that specific ritual and getting into "work mode." Over time, your brain will become more adept at shifting from a relaxed state into a productive one when it detects these cues.

Another effective work ritual involves setting an intention for the day. Before you jump into the tasks at hand, take a few minutes to reflect on your goals for the day. Whether it's reviewing your to-do list, prioritizing your tasks, or simply setting a goal for what you want to accomplish by the end of the day, having a moment of clarity helps create a sense of purpose. This intentional focus sets the tone for the work ahead and helps you avoid aimless wandering between tasks or getting distracted by irrelevant concerns.

Physical rituals can also play a significant role in transitioning into work mode. This can include something as simple as sitting in a designated chair at your desk, adjusting the lighting to your preferred level, or even engaging in a quick physical routine like a short stretch or a few minutes of deep breathing. The physical act of preparing your body in this way sends a signal to your brain that it's time to get to work. By pairing these physical actions with the mental shift into productivity, you help align your body and mind, making the transition smoother.

The environment plays a huge role in how successful your work ritual is. Making sure your workspace is organized, clutter-free, and ready for focused work is an essential part of the ritual. If your space is messy, your mind will likely feel disorganized as well. So, taking the time to clear your desk, organize files, or ensure that everything you need is within reach can prevent distractions and reduce the mental burden of trying to work in a chaotic environment.

These rituals don't have to take long. In fact, the most effective rituals are often simple and quick. Whether it's taking five minutes to review your goals, making a cup of coffee, or simply adjusting your chair to the right height, consistency is key. By performing these rituals each time you begin work, you create a habit that trains your mind to switch from a state of relaxation to a state of focus.

In short, setting up rituals to transition into work mode is about creating a predictable, comforting routine that signals to your brain that it's time to focus. These rituals don't need to be elaborate; they simply need to be consistent and tailored to what works best for you. By establishing these rituals, you reduce the friction between starting work and being productive, making it easier to dive into tasks and maintain focus throughout the day.

Controlling environmental cues.

Controlling environmental cues is an essential aspect of creating an atmosphere that supports productivity and focus. Environmental cues are the external signals in your surroundings that can influence your behavior, thoughts, and overall mental state. These cues can be physical objects, sounds, lighting, or even the arrangement of your workspace. By consciously controlling these elements, you can prime your environment to facilitate focus, minimize distractions, and increase your overall efficiency.

The first and most obvious environmental cue is the physical layout of your workspace. A cluttered or disorganized space can subconsciously create a sense of chaos or overwhelm, making it difficult to concentrate. When you eliminate unnecessary items and organize your space, you reduce visual distractions, which can help your brain stay focused on the task at hand. A clean, tidy workspace signals to your brain that it's time to work and helps keep your attention from wandering. You can enhance this further by keeping only the items relevant to the task you're working on within arm's reach, reducing the temptation to drift into other activities.

Lighting plays a crucial role in controlling environmental cues. Bright, natural light can help boost energy and alertness, while dim lighting can lead to fatigue or a relaxed mindset, making it harder to focus. Having the right lighting for your workspace can make a significant difference in how well you concentrate. If you work in a space with limited natural light, consider adding adjustable desk lamps or using light that mimics daylight to keep your energy levels up and help maintain focus. Over time, your brain will begin to associate specific lighting conditions with focused work, making it easier to slip into a productive mindset.

Another important environmental cue is noise, which can either aid or hinder your ability to concentrate. For some, background noise, like soft music or white noise, can help drown out distractions and create a more focused atmosphere. For others, absolute silence might be necessary to concentrate effectively. The key here is to identify what type of auditory environment works best for you and recreate it consistently when you need to focus. If you're in a noisy environment, noise-canceling headphones or using apps that generate calming sounds (like rain or ocean waves) can help create a more conducive workspace. Alternatively, if you need to work in silence, isolating yourself from external noises, such as turning off unnecessary electronics or finding a quiet space, can be beneficial.

Your digital environment is another powerful cue that influences productivity. Notifications, apps, emails, and social media are all digital distractions that can pull your attention away from your work. To control this, consider using productivity apps or techniques to minimize interruptions. For instance, setting your phone to "Do Not Disturb" mode or using apps that block access to distracting websites during work hours can prevent the digital noise from taking over. It's also helpful to designate specific times for checking email or social media, so these activities don't interfere with your work process.

The overall sensory atmosphere in your workspace can also impact your mental state and productivity. Aromas, for instance, can be used as environmental cues to enhance focus. Some people find that certain scents, such as peppermint or lavender, help them concentrate or relax. You might want to experiment with different scents or diffusers to see if they make a difference in your productivity. Additionally, the temperature of your workspace can play a role. Too hot or too cold environments can be distracting, so maintaining a comfortable temperature will help prevent discomfort from getting in the way of your work.

The color scheme of your workspace can also have subtle effects on your productivity. Research suggests that certain colors can influence mood and focus. For example, blue is often associated with calmness and focus, while yellow can stimulate creativity and energy. You may choose to incorporate these colors into your workspace through your decor, stationery, or wall colors. Experimenting with colors that make you feel calm, motivated, or energized can help create the ideal environment for focused work.

Finally, the presence of plants or nature in your workspace can have a positive impact on your ability to focus. Studies show that being around greenery or natural elements can reduce stress and improve cognitive function. Adding a few indoor plants or incorporating natural textures into your workspace can enhance the environment and make it more conducive to productivity.

In summary, controlling environmental cues involves consciously shaping the elements in your workspace to support focus and reduce distractions. By tailoring the lighting, noise levels, physical layout, and even sensory elements like scents and colors to your preferences, you create an environment that signals to your brain that it's time to focus. The more you optimize these cues, the more your brain will associate them with productivity, making it easier to slip into a focused state whenever you need to get to work.

9

MANAGING ENERGY TO MAXIMIZE PRODUCTIVITY

The importance of energy management

Productivity is often thought of in terms of time—how many hours you work, how many tasks you complete in a given day, and how efficiently you manage those hours. However, the real key to sustained productivity lies not just in time management, but in energy management. Time is a fixed resource, but your energy levels fluctuate throughout the day, and understanding how to harness those fluctuations can make a significant difference in your productivity. When you align your tasks with your natural energy rhythms, you can work more efficiently, feel less drained, and achieve greater results in less time.

Productivity isn't just about how many hours you work or

how much time you spend on a task. It's about managing your energy effectively and aligning your tasks with the natural rhythms of your body and mind. By recognizing when you have the most energy, scheduling your most important tasks during those times, and taking care of your physical and mental health, you can optimize your productivity and work smarter, not harder. Recognizing the importance of energy management is the key to achieving long-term success without burning out.

Why productivity isn't just about time.

Productivity is commonly associated with time, but focusing solely on time management misses a critical aspect of the equation: energy. While it's true that time is a limited resource, the quality and intensity of your output are determined by how much mental and physical energy you have to devote to a task. You can spend hours working on something, but if your energy is low, your effectiveness may decline, and the result could be subpar, or you may not complete it at all. On the other hand, when you harness your energy effectively, you can get more done in less time, and the work you produce is likely to be of higher quality.

The concept of "time management" traditionally revolves around scheduling and allocating time blocks for various tasks. However, the key challenge isn't just finding enough time to do everything; it's about making sure that when you do invest your time, you're able to bring the right amount of focus, creativity, and effort to the task at hand. When you're energized, you're more engaged, and your brain works more efficiently. This is why it's essential to prioritize energy management—by recognizing when you're most alert and focused during the day and scheduling your most demanding tasks during those times, you're setting yourself up for success.

Moreover, productivity isn't just about the number of hours you spend working but about the results you achieve during those hours. The idea that longer work hours equal more productivity often leads to burnout, mistakes, or lack of creativity. It's not about how many hours you're putting in, but about how well you're utilizing those hours. With higher energy levels, you're able to think clearer, make faster decisions, and push through challenges with greater perseverance. As a result, you can produce higher-quality work, finish tasks more efficiently, and maintain consistency over time.

Incorporating breaks, managing stress, and getting sufficient rest are critical to maintaining and restoring energy. If you're working in a depleted state, you'll likely make poor decisions, overlook important details, or experience fatigue that diminishes your ability to perform well. A well-rested, energized mind and body will be far more productive, even if you're working fewer hours, than someone who is working longer but burning out.

In essence, focusing solely on time management without considering energy management is like driving a car without checking the fuel gauge. You may be moving, but if the tank is empty, you're not going to get very far. When you balance time and energy, productivity is no longer about how long you work; it's about how effectively you use your time when you have the energy to give.

Recognizing your natural energy peaks and dips.

Recognizing your natural energy peaks and dips is crucial for optimizing productivity. Our energy levels fluctuate throughout the day, often in predictable patterns, and understanding these cycles can make a significant difference in how effectively we manage tasks.

Most people experience natural fluctuations in energy that are influenced by factors such as circadian rhythms, sleep quality, and even diet. These energy cycles are typically divided into periods of high, medium, and low energy. High energy peaks generally occur in the morning or early afternoon, depending on individual differences. During these times, people tend to feel most alert, focused, and motivated. This is when cognitive function is at its best, and it's the ideal time to tackle complex, high-concentration tasks that require problem-solving, creativity, or strategic thinking.

As the day progresses, however, many people experience an energy dip, often in the afternoon. This is sometimes referred to as the "afternoon slump" and is a common experience for those who work long hours or have irregular sleep patterns. During this period, energy levels drop, and concentration can suffer. The brain becomes less sharp, and focus tends to wander. It's a natural occurrence linked to the body's internal clock, which signals the need for rest or a break. Recognizing this dip allows you to schedule less demanding, more routine tasks during this time, such as answering emails, attending meetings, or doing tasks that don't require intense focus or creativity.

Energy levels can also dip at other times, like after a heavy meal or if a person is stressed or sleep-deprived. External factors like weather, exercise, and even your emotional state can impact these peaks and dips. For instance, if you're going through a stressful period, you may feel fatigued throughout the day, affecting your energy and productivity levels.

By recognizing your natural energy peaks and dips, you can schedule tasks in alignment with these cycles. This means working on high-concentration activities during your peak times and leaving more mundane tasks for the low-energy periods. It's not just about managing time but optimizing it by understanding when you're biologically at your best for specific types of work. Over time, this approach can help you work more efficiently, reduce procrastination, and avoid burnout.

For those who work in environments with rigid schedules or deadlines, learning to adjust your energy patterns through activities like exercise, proper nutrition, and sleep hygiene can help improve energy management. For example, taking a brief walk or stretching during an afternoon slump can give you a quick energy boost and help you recharge for the rest of the day.

Ultimately, recognizing your natural energy cycles allows you to work smarter, not harder, by leveraging your brain and body's natural rhythms. By respecting these cycles, you can avoid the frustration of pushing through tasks when your energy is low and make the most of your most productive periods.

Aligning tasks with your energy levels.

Aligning tasks with your energy levels is about strategically scheduling and prioritizing tasks to maximize your productivity throughout the day. When you become aware of your natural energy peaks and dips, you can structure your workload to ensure you're performing at your best during the times when your focus and mental capacity are at their highest. This not only helps you complete tasks more efficiently but also prevents burnout and frustration.

In the morning, many people experience their highest levels of focus and mental clarity. This is an ideal time to tackle tasks that require creativity, problem-solving, or deep concentration. Complex projects, strategic planning, or brainstorming sessions should be scheduled for this period, as your brain is fresh and capable of handling challenging cognitive tasks. During these hours, you are more likely to think critically, make sound decisions, and produce high-quality work.

Midday, your energy may start to dip slightly, especially after eating lunch. During this period, you can still maintain focus, but it's a good idea to tackle tasks that require less intense cognitive energy. These tasks might include checking and responding to emails, organizing your workspace, scheduling appointments, or performing routine administrative duties. These are tasks that don't demand deep mental engagement but still need to be done to keep things moving forward.

Later in the afternoon, many people experience another dip in energy, often resulting in a drop in concentration and motivation. Rather than pushing yourself to continue working on demanding tasks, use this time to rest, take short breaks, or engage in low-stakes activities. This might be an ideal time for light administrative work, phone calls, or creative tasks that don't require deep mental effort. Taking a brief walk or practicing mindfulness during this time can help recharge your energy and bring a burst of focus to tackle the remaining tasks.

Evening, depending on your personal rhythm, may see another surge of energy, especially if you're someone who works well late into the day. For those who feel more alert in the evening, this can be another window for deep, focused work. However, it's important to listen to your body and avoid pushing through tiredness or fatigue, as this can lead to a decrease in performance and long-term burnout.

Aligning tasks with your energy levels is also about being mindful of your physical energy. After a workout or a good night's sleep, your body will likely be rejuvenated and ready for more demanding tasks. If you've been sitting for a long time, incorporating small movement breaks throughout the day can help maintain your energy levels.

This approach allows you to match the intensity of the task with your energy availability, which improves both productivity and well-being. By consciously choosing when to tackle demanding versus more routine tasks, you're ensuring that you're not expending unnecessary mental effort when your brain isn't at its best. This prevents the need for willpower or forcing yourself to work when you're fatigued, leading to a smoother, more productive day overall.

Additionally, by aligning your tasks with your energy levels, you're optimizing your time. Rather than forcing yourself to work through a task that feels draining, you can shift focus to something that fits the energy you have at the moment. This sense of alignment helps to maintain motivation and prevents procrastination, as you're always working in sync with your natural rhythms. Over time, this approach can help you develop a sustainable and balanced work routine that maximizes both productivity and personal well-being.

Nutrition and sleep for focus

Foods that boost brain performance play a critical role in improving focus, memory, and overall cognitive function. The brain requires specific nutrients to operate at its highest capacity, and the foods you eat directly affect how well you perform mentally. A well-balanced diet rich in nutrients such as omega-3 fatty acids, antioxidants, and essential vitamins can enhance cognitive abilities, reduce mental fatigue, and improve memory retention. Omega-3s, which are found in fatty fish like salmon, walnuts, and flaxseeds, help support brain structure and function, while antioxidants from fruits like blueberries or vegetables such as spinach help protect the brain from oxidative stress. Additionally, complex carbohydrates found in whole grains provide a steady source of glucose, the brain's primary fuel, which keeps energy levels stable throughout the day.

Incorporating relaxation techniques, such as deep breathing or light stretching, before bed can help lower stress levels and prepare the body for sleep. Avoiding caffeine or heavy meals late in the day also ensures that your body isn't working against you when it's time to rest. Building a routine that includes these practices helps promote consistent, high-quality sleep, which, in turn, enhances cognitive function and provides the energy needed to stay focused throughout the day. By focusing on the importance of both nutrition and sleep, you're setting yourself up for sustained mental clarity, focus, and long-term productivity.

Foods that boost brain performance.

Foods that boost brain performance are essential for supporting cognitive functions such as memory, focus, problem-solving, and decision-making. The brain is one of the most energy-demanding organs in the body, and it relies on a steady supply of nutrients to perform at its best. Several foods are particularly effective at enhancing brain health and performance due to their high content of specific nutrients that are crucial for brain function.

Omega-3 fatty acids are among the most important nutrients for brain health. These healthy fats, particularly DHA (docosahexaenoic acid), are vital components of brain cell membranes and play a significant role in maintaining healthy brain structure and function. Omega-3 fatty acids are primarily found in fatty fish like salmon, sardines, and mackerel, but they are also present in plant-based sources such as walnuts, flaxseeds, chia seeds, and hemp seeds. Regular consumption of omega-3-rich foods has been linked to improved memory, focus, and a reduced risk of cognitive decline.

Antioxidants also play a critical role in brain performance by protecting brain cells from oxidative stress, which is caused by free radicals. Free radicals can damage brain cells, contributing to cognitive decline and conditions such as Alzheimer's disease. Foods rich in antioxidants, such as berries (blueberries, strawberries, blackberries), dark chocolate, spinach, and kale, help to neutralize free radicals and support healthy brain function. For example, blueberries are particularly effective at improving memory and cognitive function due to their high anthocyanin content, a potent antioxidant.

Vitamins and minerals are essential for supporting various brain processes, from neurotransmitter function to energy production. For instance, vitamin B12 is crucial for maintaining healthy nerve cells and producing red blood cells, which are vital for brain function. You can find vitamin B12 in animal products like eggs, meat, and dairy, as well as in fortified plant-based foods. Similarly, B vitamins, including folate (vitamin B9) and vitamin B6, are essential for synthesizing neurotransmitters like serotonin and dopamine, which influence mood and focus. Foods rich in these vitamins include leafy greens, legumes, eggs, and fortified cereals.

Complex carbohydrates provide a steady and reliable source of glucose, the brain's primary fuel. Unlike simple sugars, which cause spikes and crashes in energy, complex carbohydrates found in whole grains (such as oats, quinoa, brown rice) provide a gradual release of glucose, keeping the brain energized and focused throughout the day. Whole grains also contain fiber, which helps regulate blood sugar levels and prevents energy dips that can interfere with concentration and cognitive function.

Protein is also essential for brain performance, as it supplies amino acids that are the building blocks of neurotransmitters. Neurotransmitters are chemicals that transmit signals between brain cells, playing a significant role in regulating mood, focus, and cognitive function. Foods like lean meats, fish, eggs, tofu, and beans are excellent sources of protein, helping to support brain function by providing these essential amino acids.

Finally, staying hydrated is crucial for maintaining cognitive performance. Dehydration can lead to fatigue, poor concentration, and mental fog, making it harder to focus and think clearly. Drinking enough water throughout the day ensures that the brain stays adequately hydrated, which supports optimal cognitive function. Herbal teas and water-rich fruits and vegetables, such as cucumbers, watermelon, and oranges, also contribute to hydration and brain health.

Incorporating a variety of these nutrient-rich foods into your daily diet can significantly boost brain performance, improve memory and focus, and protect against cognitive decline. By fueling the brain with the right foods, you ensure that it has the necessary resources to function at its peak, enhancing productivity and overall mental clarity.

How sleep impacts cognitive function.

Sleep plays a critical role in maintaining and enhancing cognitive function, as it is during sleep that the brain performs essential processes that impact memory, learning, problem-solving, and decision-making. While the importance of sleep is often underestimated, it is a vital component of brain health, and the quality and quantity of sleep significantly influence how effectively the brain can perform throughout the day.

During sleep, the brain is not idle. In fact, it is incredibly active, consolidating memories, processing emotions, and cleaning up waste products that accumulate during the day. This process of memory consolidation is particularly important for learning. When we learn something new, the information is initially stored in short-term memory. However, sleep helps to transfer this information into long-term memory by strengthening neural connections. This is why getting adequate sleep after studying or acquiring new skills is crucial for retaining and recalling information.

Sleep also supports cognitive functions such as attention, focus, and decision-making. Lack of sleep impairs the brain's ability to process and retain new information, making it harder to concentrate, solve problems, and make sound judgments. Studies have shown that individuals who are sleep-deprived often struggle with tasks that require complex thinking, as well as those that demand creativity and innovation. Sleep deprivation affects the prefrontal cortex, the area of the brain responsible for higher-order thinking, planning, and decision-making. When this part of the brain is not well-rested, individuals may find themselves making impulsive or poor decisions.

Another important aspect of sleep's impact on cognitive function is its role in emotional regulation. Sleep helps the brain process emotions and recover from the stresses of the day. Without adequate rest, the brain's emotional regulation system becomes less effective, making it harder to manage stress, frustration, and anxiety. This can lead to mood swings, irritability, and difficulty focusing, which can further impair cognitive performance.

Sleep also facilitates the brain's cleaning mechanism, known as the glymphatic system. During sleep, this system helps to remove waste products from the brain, including toxic proteins like beta-amyloid, which are associated with neurodegenerative diseases like Alzheimer's. When we don't get enough sleep, the brain is unable to clear these toxins as efficiently, which over time can contribute to cognitive decline and the onset of such conditions.

Moreover, sleep is essential for maintaining mental clarity and overall brain health. Chronic sleep deprivation has been linked to a variety of cognitive issues, including memory problems, slower reaction times, and difficulty with complex thinking. It can also increase the risk of developing neurological disorders. In contrast, good sleep hygiene—consistently getting a restful night's sleep—supports brain health, reduces the risk of cognitive decline, and boosts overall cognitive performance.

Sleep quality is just as important as sleep quantity. While most adults need around 7-9 hours of sleep per night, the quality of that sleep matters. Deep sleep, or slow-wave sleep, is particularly important for cognitive functions such as memory consolidation and physical restoration. During this phase of sleep, the brain's activity is at its lowest, allowing for the most restorative benefits. Poor sleep quality, such as frequent waking or not reaching deep sleep, can prevent the brain from fully benefiting from these processes.

In sum, sleep is integral to cognitive function, impacting everything from memory and learning to decision-making and emotional regulation. By ensuring consistent, high-quality sleep, you support the brain's ability to perform optimally and maintain mental clarity, focus, and overall cognitive health. Without it, cognitive function is compromised, making it harder to stay sharp and productive throughout the day.

Creating a sleep routine for optimal energy.

Creating a sleep routine for optimal energy involves establishing consistent habits that promote deep, restful sleep, allowing the body and mind to recharge fully. Sleep is not just about the quantity of rest but also the quality, and a structured routine can significantly enhance both. By cultivating a routine that aligns with the body's natural circadian rhythms and encourages relaxation, you can improve sleep quality, boost energy levels, and enhance overall health and productivity.

The first step in creating a sleep routine is to set a consistent bedtime and wake-up time. The body's internal clock, known as the circadian rhythm, thrives on consistency. Going to bed and waking up at the same time every day, even on weekends, helps reinforce this rhythm. When your body becomes accustomed to a regular schedule, it prepares itself for sleep at the appropriate time, making it easier to fall asleep and wake up feeling refreshed. Irregular sleep patterns disrupt this rhythm, leading to poor sleep quality and increased fatigue during the day.

Next, it's important to create a pre-sleep routine that signals to the brain that it's time to wind down. This can involve engaging in relaxing activities that help ease the transition from the busyness of the day to a restful night. Activities such as reading a book, listening to calming music, practicing mindfulness, or taking a warm bath can promote relaxation. Avoid stimulating activities like using electronic devices, watching intense TV shows, or working right before bed, as these can increase mental alertness and interfere with the body's ability to relax.

The environment where you sleep plays a crucial role in the

quality of your rest. A dark, quiet, and cool bedroom creates the optimal conditions for sleep. Darkness signals to the body that it's time for rest by increasing melatonin production, a hormone that regulates sleep. If your room is too bright, especially from artificial light or streetlights, it can interfere with this process. Consider using blackout curtains or a sleep mask to block out light if necessary. Noise can also disrupt sleep, so if you live in a noisy environment, using earplugs or a white noise machine can help create a quieter, more peaceful sleeping space.

Temperature is another key factor in creating a sleep-friendly environment. The body naturally cools down during sleep, and maintaining a room temperature between 60 to 67 degrees Fahrenheit (15 to 19 degrees Celsius) can facilitate this process, helping you fall asleep more easily and enjoy deeper sleep cycles. If the room is too hot or too cold, it can disrupt sleep and cause restlessness.

Along with setting up a conducive environment, it's essential to pay attention to nutrition and hydration, particularly in the hours leading up to sleep. Avoid heavy meals, caffeine, and alcohol close to bedtime, as they can disrupt the body's ability to relax and fall asleep. Caffeine, for example, is a stimulant that can stay in the system for hours, making it harder to fall asleep. Similarly, alcohol can interfere with sleep quality by disrupting the sleep cycle and preventing deep restorative sleep.

Exercise also plays an important role in sleep quality, but timing matters. Regular physical activity can help regulate the sleep-wake cycle and improve the quality of sleep, but exercising too close to bedtime can have the opposite effect, making it harder to wind down. Ideally, aim to complete any vigorous exercise several hours before bed, allowing the body time to cool down and relax.

Creating a sleep routine that works for you requires patience and consistency, but the benefits are well worth the effort. A good sleep routine can improve mood, cognitive function, energy levels, and overall health. It also helps reduce stress, anxiety, and other factors that contribute to poor sleep, enabling you to wake up feeling rested and rejuvenated. By committing to consistent sleep habits and making your environment conducive to rest, you can ensure optimal energy throughout the day, increase your productivity, and maintain better mental and physical health over time.

Exercise and movement

Scheduling specific times for exercise can help ensure it becomes a non-negotiable part of your routine. Whether it's a morning jog, an afternoon yoga session, or an evening strength-training workout, making exercise a regular habit not only supports mental clarity but also provides a structured routine that can improve overall productivity. By committing to regular movement, you're fostering both physical and mental well-being, creating a sustainable cycle of energy, focus, and mental clarity that will benefit both your work and personal life.

The link between physical activity and mental clarity.

The connection between physical activity and mental clarity lies in the profound impact movement has on the brain. When you engage in physical activity, your heart rate increases, pumping more oxygen-rich blood to your brain. This boost in blood flow delivers essential nutrients that fuel cognitive functions such as memory, problem-solving, and decision-making. Physical activity also stimulates the production of brain-derived neurotrophic factor (BDNF), a protein that supports the growth and survival of neurons. This helps the brain create new connections, which are critical for learning and adaptability.

Regular exercise also reduces the levels of stress hormones like cortisol, which can cloud thinking and impair focus when elevated for extended periods. At the same time, physical activity prompts the release of endorphins, the brain's natural "feel-good" chemicals. These endorphins not only improve your mood but also reduce feelings of anxiety and depression, making it easier to concentrate and approach tasks with a clearer, more positive mindset.

Mental clarity is further enhanced by the ability of exercise to improve sleep quality. Deep, restorative sleep is essential for memory consolidation and cognitive function, and regular physical activity promotes better sleep patterns. This creates a virtuous cycle—better sleep enhances mental clarity, and greater clarity motivates more consistent physical activity.

In addition to these physiological effects, physical activity can serve as a mental reset. Whether it's a brisk walk, a yoga session, or a run, exercise allows you to step away from mental clutter and focus on the rhythm of your body. This "moving meditation" effect reduces overthinking and provides a fresh perspective on challenges, fostering clearer, more strategic thinking once you return to your tasks.

Aerobic exercises, in particular, are linked to significant cognitive benefits. Activities like running, swimming, or cycling not only elevate heart rate but also stimulate the release of neurochemicals that enhance attention and concentration. Meanwhile, strength training and balance-focused exercises like yoga or tai chi contribute to improved focus and stress management by teaching mindfulness and control, which carry over into your daily mental processes.

The link between physical activity and mental clarity demonstrates that moving your body isn't just beneficial for physical health—it's a cornerstone of mental performance. By making exercise a consistent part of your routine, you can create the optimal conditions for your brain to function at its best, sharpening your focus, lifting your mood, and unlocking your full cognitive potential.

Simple exercises to energize during work breaks.

Simple exercises during work breaks can be transformative for both physical energy and mental focus, offering a quick reset without disrupting your day. These short bursts of movement stimulate blood flow, release endorphins, and reduce the stiffness or fatigue that comes from prolonged sitting. By integrating brief exercises into your routine, you can re-energize your body and sharpen your mind, making it easier to tackle tasks with renewed vigor.

One of the simplest ways to recharge is through stretching.

Gentle stretches, such as reaching your arms overhead, twisting your torso side to side, or doing a seated forward bend, can relieve muscle tension and improve circulation. Stretching helps to counteract the effects of sitting for long periods, which can compress your spine and tighten your neck, shoulders, and lower back. Even a few minutes of targeted stretches can leave you feeling more relaxed and focused.

Another effective option is light cardio. Activities like brisk walking, marching in place, or climbing stairs for a couple of minutes can get your heart rate up and increase oxygen flow to your brain. These quick movements are particularly helpful for breaking through midday sluggishness. If you're working from home or in a private space, you might try jumping jacks or high knees, which are simple yet invigorating.

Strength-based exercises are another excellent choice for work breaks. Bodyweight movements like squats, wall push-ups, or lunges require no equipment and can be done almost anywhere. These exercises activate large muscle groups, helping to wake up your body and improve posture. For added benefit, you can focus on slow, controlled movements to engage your muscles fully and reduce stress.

Mind-body exercises like yoga or tai chi can also be particularly effective during breaks. A short sequence of sun salutations, for example, combines stretching, strength, and mindfulness in one fluid movement. This not only energizes your body but also calms your mind, making it easier to refocus when you return to work. Similarly, tai chi movements can be performed in a confined space and emphasize balance, coordination, and gentle flow.

Breathwork exercises can complement physical movement or serve as standalone energizers. Techniques like diaphragmatic breathing or box breathing (inhaling for four counts, holding for four counts, exhaling for four counts, and holding again) can lower stress levels and increase oxygen intake, leaving you feeling more alert and present.

Even short breaks with simple exercises can counteract the fatigue and mental fog associated with sedentary work. The key is consistency—incorporating movement into your routine throughout the day. Just five minutes of stretching, light cardio, or strength work every hour can maintain your energy levels and improve overall productivity, making each work session more effective and enjoyable.

Building movement into your daily routine.

Building movement into your daily routine is a powerful way to enhance both physical well-being and mental sharpness, helping you maintain energy levels and reduce stress through-out the day. Instead of viewing exercise as a separate, time-consuming activity, integrating it seamlessly into your daily schedule makes it more sustainable and achievable, even on the busiest days.

One effective strategy is to incorporate movement into your commute or errands. If you live close to work or local amenities, walking or biking can turn necessary travel into an opportunity for physical activity. For those who drive or take public transportation, parking further away or getting off a stop earlier allows for a short walk that invigorates you before or after your primary task. Similarly, opting for stairs instead of elevators provides a simple yet impactful way to add more movement to your day.

At work or home, you can break up long periods of sitting with micro-movements. Setting a timer to remind yourself to stand, stretch, or walk every hour can combat the negative effects of prolonged sedentary behavior. Short walks around the office, a quick trip to refill your water bottle, or even standing while taking phone calls can make a significant difference over time. Standing desks or adjustable workstations can also encourage you to alternate between sitting and standing, promoting better posture and circulation.

Routine daily activities can also double as exercise opportunities with a little creativity. For example, household chores like vacuuming, gardening, or washing the car can become a form of low-impact physical activity. These tasks not only contribute to a clean and organized environment but also keep you moving without requiring extra time or effort to "exercise."

Making movement a social activity can further enhance your routine. Scheduling regular walks with friends, family, or colleagues turns physical activity into an enjoyable and bonding experience. Group fitness classes, recreational sports, or simply playing outdoors with children or pets provide fun ways to stay active while strengthening relationships.

Technology can also play a role in embedding movement into your routine. Wearable fitness trackers or smartphone apps can remind you to move, track your activity levels, and set achievable daily step goals. These tools often gamify movement, motivating you to meet or exceed your targets. For example, a goal of 10,000 steps a day becomes more attainable when you take a few extra steps during everyday tasks.

Another approach is to incorporate movement into your leisure activities. Instead of watching TV or scrolling on your phone passively, try stretching, foam rolling, or light exercise during your screen time. Engaging in hobbies like dancing, hiking, or yoga can also add joyful movement to your day without feeling like a chore.

The key to successfully building movement into your daily routine is finding what works for you and your lifestyle. By making physical activity convenient, enjoyable, and integrated into your existing schedule, you ensure that it becomes a natural part of your day rather than an added burden. Over time, these small changes accumulate, improving your health, mood, and productivity while fostering a more active and vibrant life.

10

THE POWER OF REWARDS AND REFLECTION

Celebrating small wins

Celebrating small wins is an essential practice for maintaining motivation and building momentum toward achieving larger goals. These small victories, often overlooked in the pursuit of long-term success, serve as crucial reminders of progress and provide a sense of accomplishment that fuels further effort. When you take the time to recognize your achievements, no matter how minor they may seem, you reinforce the value of your hard work and dedication.

By celebrating small wins regularly, you create a positive feedback loop that enhances your overall mindset. It shifts your focus from solely fixating on the end goal to appreciating the journey itself. This practice not only boosts your confidence but also builds resilience, as it reminds you that progress is being made, even if it's incremental. Each celebration becomes a stepping stone, propelling you closer to your ultimate objective while keeping you engaged and inspired along the way.

Why recognition motivates further effort.

Recognition is a powerful motivator because it taps into both psychological and neurological processes that reinforce positive behavior. When you acknowledge your achievements, no matter how small, it triggers the brain's reward system, specifically the release of dopamine—a neurotransmitter associated with pleasure, motivation, and reinforcement of actions. This release creates a sense of satisfaction and accomplishment, making you more likely to repeat the behaviors that led to the achievement.

Psychologically, recognition validates your efforts, affirming that your hard work and dedication have tangible results. This affirmation is especially critical when working toward long-term goals, where the ultimate payoff might feel distant. By recognizing incremental progress, you build a sense of momentum that fuels your confidence and encourages you to persist. It's like seeing a checkpoint on a long journey; even though the destination is still ahead, knowing you've made meaningful progress keeps you energized and focused.

Recognition also meets a fundamental human need for acknowledgment and purpose. People are wired to seek validation for their actions, whether it comes from others or themselves. When you recognize your progress, you affirm that what you're doing matters and that you are capable of making meaningful strides. This validation boosts self-esteem and reinforces the belief that your efforts are worthwhile.

From a motivational perspective, recognition breaks down large, intimidating goals into manageable, rewarding steps. It shifts your focus from the overwhelming enormity of a task to the achievable milestones along the way. Each small win serves as a reminder that progress is possible, and this steady sense of achievement builds resilience against setbacks or challenges. Instead of feeling stuck or discouraged, you're encouraged to keep moving forward, knowing that every effort contributes to your overall success.

Recognition also fosters a growth mindset by emphasizing improvement and effort over perfection. When you celebrate even small accomplishments, you learn to appreciate the process and value continuous development. This mindset not only motivates further effort but also helps you navigate challenges with a more positive and constructive outlook.

In essence, recognition motivates further effort by creating a cycle of positive reinforcement, building confidence, and maintaining momentum. It transforms effort into tangible progress, energizes you to tackle the next step, and reminds you that every bit of progress, no matter how small, brings you closer to your ultimate goals.

Techniques for rewarding yourself meaningfully.

Rewarding yourself meaningfully involves creating incentives that genuinely resonate with your values, needs, and preferences, thereby reinforcing positive behavior without becoming counterproductive. The goal of a meaningful reward is to celebrate your efforts in a way that feels satisfying and encourages you to continue progressing toward your goals. This approach requires balance, intention, and alignment with what you find fulfilling.

To start, meaningful rewards are tailored to the individual. What works as a motivator for one person might not resonate with another. For some, the reward might be something tangible, like a favorite treat or a small gift. For others, it could be an experience, such as taking a long walk in nature, enjoying a relaxing bath, or watching a favorite movie. The key is to identify rewards that you genuinely enjoy and that feel like a treat, ensuring they create a positive association with the behavior or task you're reinforcing.

Timing is critical when rewarding yourself meaningfully. Immediate rewards, offered right after completing a task, are particularly effective for reinforcing behavior because they strengthen the connection between effort and gratification. For example, if you've finished a challenging project, allowing yourself a break to savor a cup of coffee or listen to your favorite playlist can serve as an instant boost of positivity. Conversely, delayed rewards can build anticipation and serve as a motivational beacon, like promising yourself a special dinner out after completing a week's worth of goals.

Another aspect of meaningful rewards is their alignment with your larger goals. The most effective rewards support your overall aspirations rather than undermining them. For instance, if you're striving for better health, celebrating with a nutritious yet indulgent meal or a new fitness gadget might be more meaningful than indulging in a habit you're trying to curb. Similarly, if financial discipline is your focus, opting for cost-free rewards, such as enjoying time with loved ones or engaging in a hobby, ensures you stay aligned with your overarching priorities.

Mindfulness and intention also play a role in creating meaningful rewards. Simply indulging in a reward without recognizing why you've earned it can dilute its impact. Taking a moment to acknowledge your accomplishment and reflect on how your efforts contributed to your progress makes the reward more satisfying. For example, after meeting a deadline, you could consciously say, "I completed this project on time, and now I'm rewarding myself with a walk to recharge."

Variety is another effective technique for meaningful rewards. Repeating the same reward for every achievement can lead to diminished satisfaction over time, a phenomenon known as reward habituation. To keep things fresh and engaging, you might alternate between different types of rewards, such as alternating between physical treats, experiences, or acts of self-care.

Lastly, combining rewards with social connection can make them even more meaningful. Sharing your success with others, such as celebrating with friends or family, not only reinforces your efforts but also strengthens bonds and provides external validation. This social acknowledgment can amplify the satisfaction you feel, motivating you to keep striving for your goals.

In summary, rewarding yourself meaningfully is about choosing incentives that resonate deeply, align with your values, and create a positive cycle of motivation. By personalizing rewards, timing them effectively, ensuring alignment with larger goals, and varying the approach, you can make the act of rewarding yourself a powerful tool for sustained productivity and growth.

Avoiding over-reliance on external rewards.

Avoiding over-reliance on external rewards involves cultivating an internal sense of motivation and fulfillment so that your drive to achieve doesn't depend entirely on outside incentives. While external rewards can be helpful for building momentum or reinforcing behavior, relying on them exclusively can limit your personal growth, reduce intrinsic motivation, and make long-term goals harder to sustain. Striking a balance between external rewards and internal satisfaction ensures you remain resilient and self-driven.

External rewards, like money, treats, or praise, provide immediate gratification, which can help kickstart new habits or encourage persistence through challenging tasks. However, if these rewards become the sole reason for your efforts, you may lose sight of the deeper, personal reasons behind your actions. For instance, someone who exercises solely to earn a reward might struggle to maintain the habit once the reward is removed. Over time, this dependency can lead to a lack of fulfillment and disengagement from the task itself.

One of the most effective ways to avoid over-reliance on external rewards is by fostering intrinsic motivation—your internal drive to perform an activity for its inherent satisfaction. This involves connecting your actions to your values, passions, or long-term goals. For example, rather than completing a project just for a bonus, focus on how mastering the skills involved contributes to your personal growth or how the task aligns with your career aspirations. Intrinsic motivation creates a sense of purpose and fulfillment, making you more likely to stick with your goals even without external incentives.

Another strategy is to gradually transition from external to internal rewards. In the beginning stages of a new habit, external rewards can be useful for building consistency and creating positive associations. Over time, shift the focus to recognizing and appreciating the internal benefits of your efforts. For instance, if you start rewarding yourself with a treat for studying, later emphasize the satisfaction of mastering the material or the pride of improving your skills. This shift helps you internalize the value of the activity itself.

Mindfulness plays a key role in avoiding over-reliance on external rewards. Regularly reflect on why you're pursuing a goal and the benefits it brings to your life. This practice helps you stay connected to the bigger picture and reinforces the intrinsic rewards of your efforts. For example, if you're working toward better fitness, pause to appreciate how exercise improves your energy, mood, and overall health, rather than just focusing on external milestones like weight loss or compliments from others.

It's also important to use external rewards sparingly and strategically. Reserve them for milestones or particularly challenging tasks rather than making them a daily necessity. This approach prevents the overuse of rewards and maintains their novelty and effectiveness. For example, celebrate significant achievements like completing a major project with a special treat, while smaller tasks are driven by the satisfaction of crossing them off your to-do list.

Balancing external rewards with self-recognition is another essential strategy. Learn to acknowledge and celebrate your achievements internally, even without tangible incentives. Take pride in your progress, however small, and reflect on the discipline, effort, or creativity you brought to a task. This self-acknowledgment nurtures self-esteem and encourages you to find joy in the process.

Cultivate habits that sustain themselves over time. When a behavior becomes automatic, it no longer requires the same level of reinforcement. For example, brushing your teeth isn't something you need a reward for; it's a habit deeply ingrained in your routine. By focusing on consistency and repetition, you can create self-sustaining behaviors that no longer depend on external rewards for motivation.

While external rewards can be useful tools, avoiding over-reliance on them ensures that your motivation remains rooted in personal satisfaction and long-term goals. By fostering intrinsic motivation, reflecting on the internal benefits of your efforts, and using external rewards sparingly, you can cultivate a sustainable and fulfilling approach to achieving your aspirations.

Reflecting on progress

Reflecting on progress is an essential practice for personal growth and sustained achievement. It provides an opportunity to pause, take stock of what you've accomplished, and evaluate the effectiveness of your strategies. This process is not just about looking back but about identifying areas of improvement and reinforcing the habits that work best for you. Reflection creates a feedback loop that enhances self-awareness and ensures that your efforts align with your goals.

Reflection is a dynamic process that evolves as you do. It's not just a one-time activity but an ongoing practice that helps you stay aligned with your goals and values. By regularly taking time to reflect, you create a habit of mindfulness and intentionality that enhances every aspect of your personal and professional life. It's a practice that not only boosts improvement but also fosters a deeper connection to your purpose and a greater appreciation for the journey itself.

How self-assessment boosts improvement.

Self-assessment is a powerful tool for personal growth and improvement because it fosters awareness, accountability, and adaptability. By evaluating your actions, decisions, and progress, you gain insights into what strategies are working and where adjustments are needed. This conscious reflection helps you break out of autopilot mode, where habits or routines might lead to stagnation, and shifts your focus toward deliberate, goal-oriented actions.

One way self-assessment boosts improvement is by promoting clarity about your strengths and weaknesses. When you take time to analyze your performance, you can identify areas where you excel and leverage those strengths more effectively. At the same time, you can pinpoint weaknesses that may be holding you back and develop targeted strategies to address them. This process transforms challenges into opportunities for growth, giving you a clearer path toward your goals.

Self-assessment also enhances accountability. By regularly checking in with yourself, you create a system of internal accountability that keeps you aligned with your objectives. It's easy to blame external factors for setbacks, but self-assessment encourages you to take ownership of your outcomes. This sense of responsibility fosters discipline and motivates you to stay on track, even when faced with obstacles or distractions.

Another key benefit is adaptability. Through self-assessment, you can evaluate how well your current strategies and habits are serving you. If something isn't working, self-reflection helps you recognize it early and make the necessary changes. This adaptability is crucial for overcoming challenges and staying resilient in the face of changing circumstances. It ensures that you remain flexible and open to new approaches, which is essential for long-term success.

Furthermore, self-assessment encourages mindfulness and intentionality. By setting aside time to reflect, you become more attuned to your thoughts, actions, and progress. This heightened awareness helps you make more thoughtful decisions and avoid impulsive behaviors that could derail your progress. Over time, this practice cultivates a deeper sense of purpose and motivation, as you see how your daily efforts contribute to your overarching goals.

Lastly, self-assessment provides a sense of achievement and satisfaction. When you look back on your progress, even small wins become visible and meaningful. Recognizing these achievements reinforces positive behaviors and builds confidence, creating a cycle of motivation and continuous improvement. It also helps you maintain perspective, reminding you of how far you've come and inspiring you to keep moving forward.

In summary, self-assessment boosts improvement by fostering clarity, accountability, adaptability, mindfulness, and a sense of accomplishment. It transforms the way you approach challenges and goals, equipping you with the tools and insights needed to grow and thrive in all areas of life.

Keeping a journal to track habits and patterns.

Keeping a journal to track habits and patterns is a simple yet transformative practice that enhances self-awareness, accountability, and personal growth. A journal acts as a mirror, reflecting not only your daily actions and routines but also the underlying thoughts, emotions, and triggers that influence them. By documenting your experiences, you create a tangible record of your behavior that can be analyzed and adjusted for improvement.

One of the key benefits of habit tracking through journaling is the ability to identify patterns. Habits, whether productive or unproductive, often occur automatically, making them difficult to notice without conscious effort. Writing down your actions helps bring these patterns to light. For example, you might discover that you're more consistent with exercising in the morning or that procrastination tends to spike when you feel overwhelmed. Recognizing these trends allows you to capitalize on your strengths and address your weaknesses with precision.

A journal also provides an effective way to measure progress. When you track your habits over time, you can see how small, consistent actions lead to significant results. This visual evidence of improvement serves as motivation, reinforcing your commitment to positive habits. It's particularly encouraging during moments when progress feels slow or stagnant, as the journal reminds you of how far you've come.

In addition to tracking habits, a journal is invaluable for

recording insights and reflections. By taking a few moments each day to note how you felt, what challenges you faced, and what you accomplished, you create a deeper connection to your goals. This reflective process helps you understand the "why" behind your habits, which is essential for sustaining long-term change. For instance, recognizing that meditation reduces your stress levels or that taking regular breaks boosts productivity strengthens your resolve to continue these practices.

Journaling also fosters mindfulness and intentionality. When you write down your goals, actions, and outcomes, you're actively engaging with the process of self-improvement rather than passively going through the motions. This heightened awareness encourages you to make deliberate choices and stay aligned with your priorities. Over time, the practice of journaling itself can become a powerful habit that supports your overall growth.

Another advantage of journaling is its ability to provide clarity during setbacks. Life is unpredictable, and even the best habits can be disrupted by unforeseen challenges. During these times, a journal serves as a tool for self-compassion and recalibration. By reflecting on what went wrong and why, you can identify strategies to overcome obstacles and prevent similar setbacks in the future. It turns failures into learning opportunities and strengthens your resilience.

Lastly, keeping a journal adds an element of celebration to habit tracking. Each entry is a testament to your effort and dedication, no matter how small the steps may seem. Reviewing past entries allows you to appreciate your journey and take pride in your accomplishments, boosting your confidence and motivation to keep going.

In essence, journaling is more than just a method for tracking habits and patterns—it's a powerful tool for personal transformation. By documenting your actions, reflecting on your experiences, and analyzing your progress, you gain the clarity, focus, and determination needed to create lasting change in your life.

Celebrating milestones, big and small.

Celebrating milestones, both big and small, is a crucial component of maintaining motivation and reinforcing positive habits. Often, we focus so much on the end goal that we forget to acknowledge the smaller steps along the way, which are just as significant. Recognizing and celebrating these moments not only boosts our morale but also helps solidify our commitment to long-term success.

When we reach a milestone, whether it's completing a challenging task, maintaining consistency with a habit, or simply making progress, it's important to take a moment to pause and appreciate the achievement. This acknowledgment serves as a reminder that progress is being made, even if it feels incremental at times. For instance, if you've been working on improving your fitness and you hit a personal best in the gym or manage to stick to a workout routine for a month, celebrating that moment reaffirms the effort and growth.

Celebrating smaller milestones is particularly powerful because it makes the journey feel less daunting. Large goals can sometimes seem overwhelming, and the path to achieving them can feel endless. By focusing on smaller achievements along the way, you break down the larger goal into more manageable steps. Each small win acts as a building block that keeps you moving forward with a sense of accomplishment and progress. It also helps maintain momentum, as the recognition of these moments fuels the drive to continue working toward the next goal.

Additionally, celebrating milestones creates a positive feedback loop. When you reward yourself for hitting a milestone, you reinforce the behaviors that led to that success. It sends a message to your brain that the effort was worthwhile, making it more likely that you will continue to engage in the actions that got you to this point. This reinforces the idea that the process of working toward a goal is just as valuable as the result itself.

Celebrating milestones also boosts your confidence. Each success, no matter how small, proves that you are capable and can achieve what you set out to do. This growing confidence is vital in overcoming setbacks or moments of self-doubt. When you encounter challenges or obstacles, you can look back at the milestones you've already achieved and use them as evidence that you can persevere and succeed again.

It's also essential to find ways to celebrate that feel meaningful and aligned with your values. For some, a small treat or a break from work might be an appropriate reward, while others might prefer to share their success with a loved one or use the milestone as an opportunity for reflection. The way you celebrate is just as important as the act of celebrating itself. It should feel authentic and rewarding in a way that reinforces the positive behavior you want to cultivate.

While it's easy to get caught up in the pursuit of the next milestone, it's important to remember that celebrations are not just about external rewards—they're also about internal validation. Taking the time to celebrate gives you the space to acknowledge the effort, the growth, and the progress you've made, fostering a sense of gratitude and satisfaction.

In conclusion, celebrating milestones is an essential practice for staying motivated and connected to the process of achieving your goals. By recognizing both the big and small achievements, you create a habit of appreciation and self-recognition that propels you toward your ultimate objectives.

11

BECOMING A PROACTIVE PERSON

Shifting your identity

Shifting your identity involves a deep transformation of how you see yourself and the role you play in your life. It's more than just adopting new habits or behaviors; it's about embracing a new self-concept. When you shift your identity, you begin to view yourself through the lens of who you want to become rather than who you have been. This change is foundational because it impacts not just what you do but how you think and feel about yourself. By shifting your identity, you start to align your actions, thoughts, and beliefs with the version of yourself you aspire to be. This shift isn't instantaneous. It's a gradual process that requires consistency, self-reflection, and the courage to break free from old patterns of thinking and behaving.

It's about moving away from labels that limit you, such as "I'm not good enough" or "I'm just not a disciplined person," and replacing them with empowering beliefs like "I am someone who can grow," or "I am capable of change." When you take on this new identity, your actions naturally start to reflect it. For example, if you see yourself as someone who values health and fitness, your daily choices will align with that identity, whether it's making healthier food choices, prioritizing exercise, or making time for self-care. Shifting your identity in this way creates a positive feedback loop—your new actions reinforce your new self-concept, and that new self-concept, in turn, fuels more positive actions.

This process also involves letting go of old stories or self-limiting beliefs that have held you back. Often, people define themselves by their past experiences or failures, which creates a barrier to growth. When you shift your identity, you rewrite the narrative. You no longer see yourself through the lens of past mistakes or missed opportunities. Instead, you embrace the idea that you are constantly evolving and that every new day offers a chance to embody the person you want to be. The power of shifting your identity lies in the realization that you have the ability to shape your future by first transforming how you view yourself. It is this inner transformation that lays the foundation for lasting, meaningful change.

Adopting the mindset of a doer.

Adopting the mindset of a doer is about shifting from a passive or reactive approach to life to one where you take proactive and consistent action. It's the difference between being someone who constantly waits for the perfect moment, motivation, or conditions to act, and being someone who understands that action itself is the key to progress. A doer doesn't wait for things to happen—they make things happen. This mindset is rooted in a sense of agency and empowerment, where you recognize that you have the ability to create change in your life, regardless of external circumstances.

When you adopt the mindset of a doer, you start to see opportunities and challenges not as obstacles, but as stepping stones to growth. The doer mindset embraces imperfection, understanding that the journey is more important than waiting for perfection. Instead of overthinking or dwelling on the potential for failure, a doer takes action anyway, learning and adjusting as they go. They don't get stuck in analysis paralysis, where they endlessly plan and think but never execute. Instead, they believe in taking imperfect action, knowing that each step, no matter how small, brings them closer to their goal.

This mindset also involves a deep commitment to persistence. A doer doesn't quit when faced with setbacks or obstacles. Instead, they keep moving forward, even if progress feels slow or difficult. They understand that success is built on a series of consistent actions over time, and they aren't deterred by short-term failures. They view mistakes as valuable lessons, using them to improve and refine their approach rather than as reasons to stop trying.

Adopting the mindset of a doer is also about taking ownership of your results. Instead of blaming circumstances or external factors for not achieving what you want, a doer takes responsibility for their actions and their outcomes. This sense of responsibility fuels motivation because it shifts the focus from things outside of your control to the power you have within yourself to create change. By seeing yourself as a doer, you are more likely to take consistent, focused action, which in turn leads to greater success and fulfillment in life.

How small changes compound over time.

Small changes may seem insignificant in the moment, but when compounded over time, they can lead to transformative results. This principle is based on the idea that progress isn't always about making drastic, immediate shifts, but rather about making steady, consistent improvements. When you make small, positive changes and stick to them, they accumulate, creating a snowball effect that leads to exponential growth.

Consider how making just one small change—like drinking an extra glass of water each day—may not feel like a big deal at first. However, over weeks, months, and years, those extra glasses of water add up to a significant improvement in hydration, energy, and health. Similarly, committing to just 10 minutes of exercise a day may seem like a small effort, but over time, it can dramatically improve your fitness levels, increase your energy, and improve your mental health.

The key to this process is consistency. Small changes that are repeated daily, without interruption, accumulate into something far greater than the sum of their parts. The impact of a single action might not be noticeable right away, but over time, those small actions become habits, and those habits shape your behaviors, mindset, and ultimately your life.

This principle also works in the opposite direction: small negative changes, when compounded over time, can lead to undesirable outcomes. If you continually skip healthy meals, for example, the small choice of eating something unhealthy may not seem like much in the moment, but over time, it can result in negative health outcomes.

By focusing on small, incremental improvements, you can avoid feeling overwhelmed by the need to make huge, life-altering changes. Instead, you focus on manageable actions that, when practiced consistently, lead to lasting change. This approach helps to build momentum, as success in small areas boosts confidence, which then fuels more positive change in other areas. Over time, these small changes become the foundation for achieving big goals and making lasting improvements in your life.

Reframing challenges as opportunities.

Reframing challenges as opportunities is about shifting your perspective on obstacles, difficulties, or setbacks in a way that encourages growth, learning, and positive action. Instead of viewing challenges as roadblocks or failures, you start to see them as stepping stones that provide valuable lessons and opportunities for personal development.

This mindset shift is powerful because it helps you move away from fear and frustration, which often come with facing difficulties, and instead fosters a sense of curiosity and resilience. When you reframe challenges, you're no longer paralyzed by them; instead, you approach them with the mindset that they are opportunities to improve, innovate, and grow stronger.

For example, if you're faced with a challenging project at work, instead of feeling overwhelmed by the complexity or doubting your abilities, you can view it as a chance to learn new skills, improve problem-solving abilities, and gain experience that will be valuable in the future. Rather than seeing the situation as something that could make you fail, you can see it as an opportunity to succeed in a way that's only possible through overcoming difficulty.

Similarly, setbacks in personal life, like a missed deadline or a mistake, can be reframed as valuable feedback. These challenges provide information about areas that need improvement and guide you toward strategies that can help you do better next time. This reframing doesn't mean ignoring the discomfort or frustration that comes with challenges, but it allows you to process those emotions more productively, finding purpose and meaning in the struggle.

Reframing challenges as opportunities also enables you to stay motivated. When you focus on what you can learn and how you can grow from a tough situation, you're more likely to keep going and push through obstacles. This approach fosters a sense of empowerment, as you begin to view challenges not as hindrances to your goals but as catalysts for positive change.

In essence, reframing challenges as opportunities allows you to cultivate a growth mindset. You stop seeing yourself as a passive recipient of life's difficulties and instead become an active participant, using each challenge as an opportunity to evolve into a stronger, more capable version of yourself.

Embracing action-oriented habits

Embracing action-oriented habits means committing to a way of living where taking initiative and consistently moving forward becomes second nature. Rather than waiting for motivation to strike or letting external circumstances dictate when action is taken, individuals with action-oriented habits actively choose to take the first step, no matter how small, every day. This mindset leads to a shift in how tasks, goals, and opportunities are approached. It's about developing a proactive stance on life where action, rather than inaction, becomes the default response to challenges.

Embracing action-oriented habits isn't about perfection; it's about consistency. It's about making progress every day, even if it's just a small step, and reinforcing the mindset that action is the key to overcoming obstacles and achieving goals. By turning proactive behavior into a lifestyle, sustaining long-term productivity, and avoiding relapse into procrastination patterns, you can create a momentum that will carry you toward success, no matter the challenges you face.

Turning proactive behavior into a lifestyle.

Turning proactive behavior into a lifestyle involves adopting a mindset and daily habits that prioritize taking action, anticipating challenges, and making intentional progress, regardless of how small the steps might seem. This shift requires moving away from a reactive mode, where you respond to circumstances as they come, and instead embracing a proactive approach where you anticipate needs, solve problems before they escalate, and stay ahead of the curve.

It starts with recognizing that waiting for motivation or the "right time" often leads to missed opportunities and stagnation. Proactive individuals take the lead in their lives by setting goals, planning ahead, and making decisions based on their values and priorities rather than waiting for external circumstances to dictate their actions. This shift from waiting to doing requires you to be self-motivated, forward-thinking, and willing to step out of your comfort zone regularly.

To turn this behavior into a lifestyle, it's essential to weave proactive actions into daily routines. For example, starting each day by identifying one key task to focus on, planning ahead for potential challenges, or even doing a quick review of upcoming commitments can set the tone for being in control of your day. It can also involve setting regular reminders to check in on long-term goals, break down bigger projects into smaller tasks, and commit to taking one meaningful action toward them every day.

Small, consistent steps are the foundation for making proactive behavior a lifestyle. By taking ownership of the outcomes in your life, you stop waiting for things to happen and start making them happen. You also build resilience against setbacks because you've trained yourself to act first, rather than being paralyzed by fear, indecision, or overwhelm. Over time, being proactive becomes less about making grand efforts and more about consistently showing up, solving problems early, and making continuous, incremental progress. This mindset shift, combined with habitual action, forms the foundation for living a life of intentionality and forward momentum.

Strategies to sustain long-term productivity.

Sustaining long-term productivity requires more than just short bursts of effort; it's about creating habits, routines, and mindsets that consistently support and nurture focus, motivation, and efficiency over time. To make productivity sustainable, the strategies must account for not only the work itself but also the need for balance, self-care, and adaptability.

One strategy for long-term productivity is to establish clear, meaningful goals that are broken down into smaller, manageable tasks. This makes it easier to stay focused and on track without becoming overwhelmed by the bigger picture. By setting both short-term and long-term goals, you create a roadmap that helps you measure progress and maintain momentum. It's also crucial to make sure these goals are aligned with your values and priorities, ensuring that the work you're doing remains motivating and meaningful.

Another important strategy is regular time management, which involves prioritizing tasks and allocating your energy wisely. One effective approach is time blocking—setting aside specific blocks of time for different tasks or types of work. This helps to prevent decision fatigue and ensures you are dedicating focused time to the most important activities. Building flexibility into your schedule also plays a key role in maintaining long-term productivity, as it allows for unexpected interruptions or shifts without derailing your progress.

Equally important is the practice of self-care and regular breaks. Working without rest leads to burnout, and this is one of the biggest threats to long-term productivity. The brain needs time to recharge, and taking regular breaks throughout the day helps maintain mental clarity and prevent fatigue. This can be achieved through techniques like the Pomodoro method, which encourages alternating periods of focused work with short breaks. Additionally, ensuring you get enough sleep, exercise, and nutrition is crucial for sustaining productivity levels.

Another strategy is fostering a growth mindset and embracing the idea that setbacks are opportunities for learning rather than failures. By viewing challenges and mistakes as stepping stones rather than roadblocks, you maintain motivation and the resilience to continue pushing forward, even during difficult times.

Finally, to sustain productivity in the long run, it's important to periodically reassess and adjust your approach. What worked for you a year ago may not work today, so being willing to adapt, refine your strategies, and try new tools or methods ensures that your productivity remains effective and enjoyable.

Long-term productivity isn't about working harder; it's about working smarter, maintaining balance, and continuously optimizing your strategies to stay aligned with your goals and values. By building these habits and routines, you ensure that you're not just productive today, but you're creating a sustainable approach that keeps you efficient and motivated for the long haul.

Avoiding relapse into procrastination patterns.

Avoiding relapse into procrastination patterns is a key part of maintaining long-term productivity. It requires awareness, intentionality, and consistent action to stay on track, even when the temptation to delay tasks arises. Procrastination often emerges from deeper psychological factors like fear of failure, perfectionism, or overwhelming tasks, so combating it is not just about pushing through laziness—it's about addressing the underlying triggers and creating habits that discourage procrastination.

The first step in avoiding relapse is recognizing the warning signs of procrastination before they become ingrained habits again. This requires self-awareness. By noticing when you begin to feel resistant to starting tasks—whether it's because they seem too daunting, uninteresting, or you're simply feeling overwhelmed—you can intervene early. For example, recognizing that you're avoiding a task by checking social media or organizing things obsessively can serve as a signal to step back and reassess. Identifying these avoidance behaviors allows you to catch them before they snowball into more significant procrastination.

Next, one effective way to prevent procrastination is to break tasks into smaller, more manageable steps. Large, intimidating projects often trigger procrastination because they feel insurmountable. By dividing tasks into small, bite-sized actions, you make them feel more achievable. For instance, rather than saying, "I need to write this report," break it down into subtasks like researching, outlining, drafting sections, and proofreading. Each of these individual steps feels more attainable and manageable, which reduces the chances of procrastination taking hold.

Another approach is to focus on building strong routines that make productivity a habit rather than a struggle. When you have set work periods, designated tasks, and a consistent approach to managing your time, the decision to work becomes automatic. Creating structure and predictable patterns in your day helps reduce the mental burden of deciding when and how to work. When you remove the uncertainty and decision fatigue, there's less room for procrastination to thrive.

It's also essential to change the way you perceive tasks. Often, procrastination arises from a fear of failure or a desire for perfectionism. Shifting your mindset from a perfectionist viewpoint to a focus on progress rather than perfection helps mitigate these barriers. Instead of expecting a flawless outcome, remind yourself that the goal is to simply get started, make progress, and adjust as you go. Understanding that mistakes are part of the learning process can help reduce the fear that leads to procrastination.

Additionally, setting time limits and using techniques like the Pomodoro Technique—working in focused intervals followed by short breaks—can help you avoid overwhelm and stay engaged with the task at hand. This structure creates a sense of urgency while also allowing for mental rest, which prevents burnout and stagnation.

Accountability plays a key role in combating procrastination too. By having an accountability partner or a system to track your progress, you introduce external motivation to stay on task. Regular check-ins or setting small milestones can provide the encouragement needed to stay on course, particularly when procrastination tendencies begin to resurface.

Lastly, it's important to practice self-compassion and not beat yourself up when a procrastination slip-up happens. Perfection is not the goal; persistence is. Be kind to yourself, reflect on what caused the setback, and adjust accordingly without judgment. By fostering a positive mindset and a growth-oriented perspective, you're better equipped to recognize when procrastination reappears, and you can quickly get back on track.

Ultimately, avoiding relapse into procrastination requires a combination of self-awareness, proactive planning, emotional management, and establishing a consistent routine. By making productivity a habit, reducing task anxiety, and fostering accountability, you can prevent procrastination from regaining control over your time and focus.

Inspiring others to change

Sharing your success story can be a powerful tool in inspiring others to change. When you openly talk about how you've overcome procrastination and transformed your own habits, it not only validates the possibility of change but also shows others that it's achievable. People are more likely to take action when they see someone they relate to succeed, especially if they can connect with the struggles and challenges you've faced. By telling your story, you provide tangible proof that change is possible, and your experience becomes a blueprint for others to follow. It's not about boasting; it's about showing vulnerability and offering hope to those who may feel stuck in their own procrastination habits. Your journey becomes a source of inspiration and motivation, sparking the desire in others to take control of their habits and push past their own barriers.

Sharing your success story.

Sharing your success story can have a profound impact on both yourself and others. When you take the time to reflect on how far you've come, you not only celebrate your own achievements but also create a ripple effect of motivation for those who may be struggling with similar challenges. Your journey, filled with both successes and setbacks, becomes a roadmap for others who may feel lost in their own efforts. It serves as a reminder that change is possible, and it is not always immediate. Often, people need to see tangible examples of others' success to truly believe in their own potential for growth. By openly sharing the highs and lows of your process, you humanize the struggle and show others that overcoming obstacles is part of the journey—not a sign of failure.

When you share how you overcame procrastination, you provide others with insights into the specific strategies and habits that worked for you. Your story can include practical steps that others can implement in their own lives, like setting achievable goals, practicing self-discipline, or embracing the small wins along the way. You can also share the mindset shifts that helped you, such as learning to see failure as a stepping stone rather than a roadblock or understanding the power of consistent, incremental progress.

Additionally, telling your success story fosters a sense of connection. Many people battling procrastination feel isolated, believing that they are the only ones struggling. Hearing someone else's story can help break down that isolation, showing them they are not alone. It helps shift the focus from the difficulty of the task to the possibility of success. Moreover, your story becomes a source of inspiration that encourages others to take action, to try new strategies, and to believe that they, too, can succeed. When you openly discuss how you overcame your procrastination habits, you offer a beacon of hope to others and create a sense of community where people can come together to support one another in their personal growth.

Supporting friends and family in overcoming procrastination.

Supporting friends and family in overcoming procrastination requires a balance of empathy, encouragement, and practical advice. Procrastination often stems from deeper psychological factors like fear of failure, perfectionism, or a lack of confidence. As someone who has navigated these challenges, you can offer valuable insight, but the key to helping others is understanding their individual struggles without judgment. When you support those close to you, it's important to listen actively to their concerns and acknowledge their feelings, showing them that they are not alone in facing these difficulties.

Rather than simply offering solutions, begin by creating a safe space for open communication. Many people who struggle with procrastination may feel ashamed or embarrassed about their habits. By letting them know that it's okay to experience setbacks and that overcoming procrastination is a gradual process, you foster an atmosphere of trust. When people feel heard and understood, they are more likely to open up about their struggles and be receptive to the advice or strategies you share.

Practical guidance is often helpful, but it needs to be tailored to the individual. Suggesting techniques such as breaking tasks into smaller steps, using reminders, or setting achievable goals can give your friends and family the tools they need to take action. Encourage them to celebrate small victories along the way, as this helps build momentum and reinforces positive behavior. Additionally, you can help them recognize their natural energy peaks and dips, suggesting they align challenging tasks with their most focused times of day.

Another important aspect of supporting others is fostering accountability. Gently check in with them to see how they're doing, not as a way of policing their progress, but as a means of offering encouragement and tracking their growth. You can suggest that they set up accountability systems, whether through regular check-ins with you or with other support networks.

However, it's also essential to respect their pace and not pressure them to change too quickly. Transformation takes time, and even small setbacks can feel discouraging. Help them reframe these moments as opportunities for learning, rather than failure. Remind them that the process is ongoing and that every step forward, no matter how small, is a victory.

By being patient, empathetic, and proactive, you can be an influential source of support for your friends and family in overcoming procrastination. Your encouragement can make all the difference in helping them build confidence, embrace healthier habits, and take consistent action toward their goals.

Building a community of action-takers.

Building a community of action-takers is about creating a supportive and motivating environment where individuals hold each other accountable and encourage consistent progress. It's not just about finding people with similar goals, but rather about fostering a culture of action, where everyone is committed to moving forward and tackling their tasks with purpose.

The first step in creating such a community is establishing a shared vision or purpose. This helps to ensure that everyone is aligned in their objectives, whether it's overcoming procrastination, improving productivity, or achieving personal goals. The collective energy and focus that come from being part of a community with a common goal can be incredibly motivating. When people see others taking action and making progress, it serves as a reminder that their own efforts are part of something bigger, creating a ripple effect of action and momentum.

Regular interaction is key in keeping the community engaged and active. This can be achieved through weekly meetings, virtual check-ins, or group chats where everyone shares their goals, progress, and setbacks. Having a space for these discussions creates a sense of accountability. Knowing that others are counting on you to follow through can provide the extra push needed to get things done. It also creates an opportunity to celebrate wins together, which fosters a sense of accomplishment and strengthens the community bond.

Moreover, a community of action-takers thrives on mutual support and encouragement. When someone faces a setback or struggles to stay motivated, others can offer advice, share their own experiences, or simply provide emotional support. This sense of solidarity can make a huge difference in overcoming obstacles. Knowing that you're not alone in your challenges can be a powerful motivator. It helps people feel understood and validated, making it easier to continue pushing forward.

In addition to support and accountability, it's important to establish a system of shared resources. This could include tools, strategies, or even courses that members of the community can benefit from. By pooling knowledge and resources, the community creates an environment where everyone is continuously learning and growing together. This shared knowledge helps keep the momentum going, as each member gains new insights and approaches that can improve their productivity and action-taking.

It's also essential to maintain a positive and growth-focused mindset within the community. There should be a culture of celebrating progress, no matter how small, and reframing setbacks as learning opportunities rather than failures. This ensures that people don't get discouraged if they stumble along the way and that they remain committed to their goals.

Finally, a community of action-takers is not just about motivation but also about consistency. Encourage the group to develop habits and routines that support their goals and make action-taking a part of their everyday life. This can include setting aside dedicated time for goal-related tasks, tracking progress, and creating systems that foster productivity. When these habits become ingrained, they propel individuals forward with little effort, turning action into a natural part of their daily routine.

By building a community that prioritizes action, accountability, and mutual support, you create an environment where everyone feels empowered to achieve their goals. The shared experiences, encouragement, and tools available within such a community serve to reinforce the habits of successful action-takers and promote long-term growth and progress for all involved.

12

BONUS

Your Journey Beyond Procrastination

Embarking on the journey to overcome procrastination is not just about learning new strategies or applying different techniques—it's about transformation. It's about shifting from a life of delay, stress, and unfulfilled potential to one of consistent action, productivity, and self-empowerment. The journey beyond procrastination is deeply personal and unique for every individual, but it is universally rooted in self-awareness, mindset change, and the cultivation of lasting habits. This book has equipped you with the tools, insights, and strategies to begin this journey, but the real work starts now.

Procrastination, at its core, is often a barrier built by fear, self-doubt, and emotional resistance. It is not merely a habit of putting things off; it's a reaction to discomfort, an avoidance of tasks that trigger negative feelings or require significant mental effort. This book has explored the science behind procrastination—the emotional and psychological triggers that feed it—and introduced you to methods of identifying, confronting, and dismantling those triggers. The journey beyond procrastination, therefore, is less about trying to eradicate procrastination entirely and more about learning how to respond to it differently.

The First Step: Understanding Procrastination as a Mindset

Procrastination is often thought of as a time-management problem, but it's much more than that. It's a mindset issue, and that mindset is shaped by the way we perceive tasks, emotions, and ourselves. A major part of the journey is recognizing that procrastination is not a moral failing but a product of cognitive and emotional responses. When we experience feelings of anxiety, fear, or perfectionism, our brains are wired to avoid the discomfort those feelings bring. Overcoming procrastination requires us to confront these fears head-on and shift our thinking about tasks and deadlines.

This mindset shift involves recognizing that procrastination isn't a matter of laziness or poor self-discipline. It's often a self-protective mechanism against emotional pain or discomfort. And, once we begin to view procrastination in this light, we can approach it with compassion and curiosity instead of self-criticism. The journey beyond procrastination begins when we stop seeing ourselves as failures because we procrastinate, and start recognizing procrastination as an opportunity for growth, learning, and self-improvement.

The Power of Self-Awareness and Reflection

Self-awareness is a crucial component of overcoming procrastination. To move beyond it, you must first take the time to observe your patterns, triggers, and thoughts that fuel procrastination. Where do you typically procrastinate? Which tasks do you avoid the most? What emotions arise when you think about getting started on a project? By asking yourself these questions and reflecting on the answers, you can begin to identify the root causes of your procrastination.

Building self-awareness involves examining not just your behaviors, but the emotions and thoughts behind them. For example, if you consistently delay starting a project because you fear it won't be perfect, this points to perfectionism as a barrier to action. If you tend to procrastinate when you feel overwhelmed, this suggests that breaking tasks down into smaller, more manageable steps might be the key to overcoming that hurdle. The more you understand your triggers, the better equipped you'll be to make intentional, strategic choices that move you beyond procrastination.

This book has laid the foundation for this self-reflection, but it's your responsibility to continue the practice of journaling, evaluating your behavior, and setting new goals. The more you reflect on your progress, the clearer the path becomes. Reflection is not just about looking back on mistakes, but about gaining clarity on what has worked and what hasn't. It's about identifying your strengths and weaknesses, learning from both, and using those lessons to fuel your future efforts.

Building New Habits and Routines

As you move beyond procrastination, you'll find that building new, productive habits is at the heart of lasting change. Procrastination is a habit—a cycle of avoidance, stress, and guilt. Breaking free from this cycle requires replacing it with more empowering habits that support your goals and align with your values. These new habits won't appear overnight, but with consistent practice, they will gradually become part of your daily routine.

The book has provided numerous techniques to help you develop better habits, such as using productivity tools, setting up systems to stay organized, and incorporating physical activity and mindfulness into your routine. The key to success lies in small, consistent steps. By choosing to take action—no matter how small—on a daily basis, you begin to rewire your brain to seek action over avoidance. This gradual, sustained effort leads to lasting transformation.

It's important to understand that the process of habit formation is not linear. There will be days when you slip back into old patterns or face new challenges that make it harder to stay on track. But the key is to be patient with yourself, to keep moving forward, and to understand that each small step builds upon the last. You are laying the foundation for a new way of living—one where procrastination no longer has the power to control your actions or your future.

Embracing the Power of Action

At some point, the shift beyond procrastination becomes an active choice—a choice to embrace action. For many people, the hardest part of overcoming procrastination is simply getting started. Once you take that first step, momentum begins to build. The key is to create a system of action that doesn't depend on motivation or mood. By using the strategies outlined in this book, such as setting clear intentions, focusing on one task at a time, and breaking down large projects into manageable chunks, you can eliminate the friction that typically causes you to procrastinate.

The more you practice this proactive behavior, the easier

it becomes to take action when faced with new challenges or tasks. You'll find that instead of waiting for motivation to strike, you can create your own momentum by simply starting. Action breeds action. As you progress on your journey, you'll develop an internal sense of discipline and drive that becomes your default way of operating, pushing procrastination further out of the picture.

Reframing Challenges and Celebrating Progress

Another crucial aspect of moving beyond procrastination is how you frame challenges. Procrastination often arises from a negative perception of tasks—seeing them as daunting, overwhelming, or unpleasant. To truly break free, you must reframe these challenges as opportunities for growth, learning, and achievement. This shift in perspective allows you to approach tasks with a mindset of curiosity rather than dread.

Each task you complete, no matter how small, is a victory—a proof of your ability to take action despite fear, doubt, or discomfort. This book has emphasized the importance of celebrating small wins, and this is a key part of your journey. The more you acknowledge your progress, the more you reinforce your new habits and build the confidence needed to tackle even bigger tasks.

Your journey beyond procrastination is not just about productivity—it's about personal growth. It's about recognizing that procrastination is merely a phase in your development, and that you have the power to transcend it. With the tools, insights, and strategies shared in this book, you now have the ability to break free from procrastination's grip and unlock your potential for success.

Moving Forward with Confidence

As you move beyond procrastination, remember that this is a

lifelong journey. The habits and mindset you've developed will serve you in all areas of life, helping you tackle new challenges, reach new goals, and continue growing as a person. With each step, you'll build the confidence and resilience necessary to achieve lasting success.

Thank you for taking this journey with me. Your commitment to moving beyond procrastination is an important first step in creating a more fulfilling, productive life. As you continue on this path, know that every action you take brings you closer to becoming the person you want to be—a person who doesn't just dream of success but actively creates it every day.

13

WHAT DISTINGUISH THE BOOK FROM OTHER BOOKS

When it comes to tackling procrastination, the market is flooded with self-help books offering a range of quick tips, motivational quotes, and strategies that promise to "fix" procrastination overnight. But here's the truth: overcoming procrastination is not about a simple, one-size-fits-all solution. It requires understanding the deeper psychological mechanisms at play, creating a sustainable system of change, and committing to long-term, meaningful progress. *Procrastination Unlocked* stands apart from the sea of other books because it doesn't just skim the surface of procrastination—it goes deep into the science behind it, offering real, research-backed methods to help you break the cycle and unlock your true potential.

1. Rooted in Science and Psychology

Unlike many self-help books that rely on vague, surface-level advice or motivational platitudes, *Procrastination Unlocked* is grounded in the latest psychological research. The book delves into why procrastination happens, identifying the cognitive biases, emotional responses, and environmental factors that drive us to delay important tasks. By understanding the true causes of procrastination—rather than just treating its symptoms—you'll be able to tackle the issue from a place of knowledge and insight. This scientific foundation sets the book apart from other titles that often oversimplify the process of change.

Through a deep exploration of neuroscience, cognitive-behavioral theories, and emotional regulation strategies, you'll learn exactly what is happening in your brain when you procrastinate. It's not about lazy habits or weak willpower; it's about understanding the way your mind works and using that knowledge to reprogram your behavior.

2. Practical, Actionable Strategies with Long-Term Impact

Many books offer quick tips to "get more done," but often those tips don't stick. They are fleeting solutions, providing temporary relief but not addressing the root cause of procrastination. What makes *Procrastination Unlocked* unique is its emphasis on sustainable, long-term change. It offers actionable strategies that are designed not only to help you stop procrastinating now but also to cultivate habits that will keep you productive in the long run.

We don't just focus on time management tricks like using to-do lists, calendars, or productivity apps. We go deeper—helping you create systems for your life that work with your natural rhythms, mental states, and energy levels. You'll learn how to design a workspace that nurtures focus, build routines that reduce decision fatigue, and create a sleep and exercise plan that fuels your brain and body. This holistic approach allows you to integrate productivity into every aspect of your life, making it easier to sustain your efforts.

3. Focus on Developing a Productive Mindset

Many books approach procrastination as a problem to be "fixed," but *Procrastination Unlocked* focuses on the mindset shifts that are crucial to overcoming procrastination for good. It's not just about learning how to manage your time or creating an ideal work environment—it's about developing the mindset of a doer. The book shows you how to reframe challenges as opportunities, build confidence in your ability to take action, and embrace small, consistent changes that compound over time.

Procrastination is often rooted in self-doubt, fear of failure, and perfectionism. Instead of offering generic advice on how to "push through" or "just do it," this book empowers you to shift your entire perspective. You'll learn how to replace the inner narratives that keep you stuck with healthier, more productive ways of thinking. By fostering a mindset centered around action, you'll start to see productivity as a natural part of who you are rather than a battle against your own mind.

4. Integrating Mindfulness and Emotional Intelligence

Another standout feature of *Procrastination Unlocked* is its integration of mindfulness practices and emotional intelligence techniques. Many productivity books fail to address the emotional and psychological underpinnings of procrastination. But procrastination isn't just a lack of time management—it's often an emotional reaction to stress, anxiety, or fear. By incorporating mindfulness practices, the book teaches you how to stay present, manage overwhelming emotions, and build emotional resilience.

You'll learn how to use mindfulness to reduce procrastination triggers, manage negative thoughts, and stay focused on the present moment. This is a crucial skill for breaking the procrastination cycle. Rather than avoiding the difficult feelings associated with tasks, mindfulness empowers you to face them head-on without retreating into delay. This emotional awareness isn't just about managing feelings; it's about using those feelings to create better, more productive habits.

5. Personalized and Flexible Approach

Every person is different, and what works for one individual may not work for another. *Procrastination Unlocked* recognizes that there is no single, one-size-fits-all solution to procrastination. It offers a flexible framework that can be customized to suit your unique needs, lifestyle, and goals. Whether you struggle with decision fatigue, lack of motivation, or poor time management, you'll find specific strategies tailored to your personal challenges.

The book doesn't present a rigid, prescriptive approach. Instead, it encourages you to experiment with various tools and strategies to find what works best for you. Whether it's time-blocking, building momentum through small tasks, or using productivity apps, you'll have the flexibility to adapt these methods in ways that suit your own workflow and personality.

6. Focus on Building Lasting Habits, Not Quick Fixes

One of the biggest criticisms of many productivity books is their focus on quick fixes that offer temporary solutions but fail to produce lasting change. *Procrastination Unlocked* takes the opposite approach. Instead of providing short-term hacks or tricks to get through a project, the book emphasizes building lasting habits that will support your productivity for a lifetime.

By focusing on habit formation, self-discipline, and emotional regulation, the book equips you with the tools to make lasting changes. Through practical exercises, real-life examples, and step-by-step guidance, you'll learn how to build habits that naturally lead to greater focus, motivation, and success. This isn't about grinding through tasks—this is about creating a lifestyle where productivity comes easily and effortlessly.

7. Holistic Approach to Productivity

Procrastination Unlocked is more than just a book on overcoming procrastination—it's a comprehensive guide to living a productive, balanced life. The book delves into topics that are often overlooked in other productivity guides, such as the importance of nutrition, sleep, and exercise for mental clarity and focus. By providing strategies for optimizing your body and mind, it ensures that you have the energy and resilience necessary to tackle your goals with confidence.

In addition, the book emphasizes the importance of self-reflection, celebrating small wins, and continuously improving. By adopting a growth mindset and focusing on progress rather than perfection, you'll develop the self-awareness and confidence needed to stay on track over time.

Procrastination Unlocked stands apart from other books on the subject because it goes beyond surface-level strategies and offers a deep, scientifically-backed, and holistic approach to overcoming procrastination. By focusing on understanding the psychology behind procrastination, developing a proactive mindset, and building lasting habits, this book equips you with everything you need to finally break free from procrastination. Whether you're struggling with time management, focus, motivation, or emotional regulation, you'll find practical, actionable strategies that are tailored to your personal needs.

This book isn't just about getting things done today—it's about transforming your relationship with work and productivity, allowing you to achieve lasting success in all areas of your life. By choosing *Procrastination Unlocked*, you've taken the first step toward unlocking your potential, and with the knowledge and strategies you've gained, there's nothing stopping you from achieving greatness.

14

CONCLUSION

Congratulations! You've made it to the end of *Procrastination Unlocked: The Science Behind Getting Things Done*. This marks the beginning of your transformation from a procrastinator to a focused and productive individual. Throughout this book, we've explored the psychology behind procrastination, offering insights into why we delay, and how it affects our lives in ways we might not even realize. Most importantly, we've provided you with actionable strategies to break free from this cycle and create lasting habits that will propel you toward success.

Your journey beyond procrastination starts with understanding that procrastination isn't just a bad habit—it's a complex issue driven by emotions, cognitive biases, and our brain's natural tendency to seek comfort. But armed with knowledge, you now know that procrastination can be overcome. We've talked about the science behind time management, focus, decision-making, and energy levels. More importantly, you've learned how to apply practical techniques like time-blocking, setting up routines, building willpower, and embracing mindfulness to take control of your time.

What sets this book apart from others is its approach. Rather than just offering quick fixes or temporary solutions, we've focused on the root causes of procrastination and provided a sustainable framework for long-term productivity. Whether it's creating a workspace that promotes focus, harnessing the power of self-discipline, or using mindfulness and nutrition to keep your energy levels high, this book integrates science-backed strategies with practical tools. It's not about just getting things done in the short term; it's about changing your habits and mindset for good, transforming the way you approach challenges, and cultivating a new relationship with work.

By now, you should feel equipped with the tools, knowledge, and strategies you need to take action and stop procrastinating. But remember, the key to success is consistent effort and practice. The journey doesn't end here—each step you take towards overcoming procrastination is a step towards a more productive, fulfilling life.

I sincerely appreciate you taking the time to read this book. Your commitment to improving your habits and breaking free from procrastination is commendable. If you found value in these pages, I would be incredibly grateful if you could share your experience by leaving a review on Amazon. Your feedback not only helps others find this book but also motivates me to continue creating helpful content.

15

QUIZ SECTION

What is the primary psychological trigger for procrastination?

How does emotional resistance contribute to procrastination?

What is the difference between procrastination and relaxation?

Explain why self-awareness is crucial in overcoming procrastination.

What role does fear of failure play in procrastination?

Describe how perfectionism can lead to delaying tasks.

What is the connection between stress and procrastination?

How does dopamine influence procrastination behavior?

Why is it important to focus on progress over perfection?

What is the "two-minute rule" and how can it help combat procrastination?

Explain how breaking down large tasks into smaller steps can reduce procrastination.

What is the purpose of creating a clear action plan?

How does setting deadlines impact productivity?

Why should you prioritize tasks based on urgency and importance?

How can recognizing your natural energy levels help you work more effectively?

Describe the impact of a cluttered workspace on procrastination.

How can removing distractions improve focus and productivity?

Why is it important to control environmental cues when fighting procrastination?

What foods are known to enhance brain performance and focus?

How does proper hydration impact cognitive function?

What is the relationship between sleep and productivity?

How does a consistent sleep routine improve focus and energy levels?

Name one exercise you can do during a work break to re-energize.

What are the mental benefits of regular physical activity?

How can journaling help track habits and progress?

Why is it important to celebrate small wins in the fight against procrastination?

What is the potential downside of relying too heavily on external rewards?

How does self-assessment contribute to personal improvement?

Why is progress often non-linear, and how should setbacks

be viewed?

What is the significance of lifelong learning in overcoming procrastination?

How do small, consistent changes compound into larger transformations?

What is the importance of reframing challenges as opportunities?

How can adopting the mindset of a "doer" help you stay productive?

Why is building action-oriented habits critical to long-term success?

How can creating systems help sustain long-term productivity?

What strategies can help prevent a relapse into procrastination patterns?

Why is sharing your success story beneficial for others and yourself?

How can you support friends and family in overcoming procrastination?

What are the benefits of building a community of action-takers?

Why is it important to reflect on your personal journey beyond procrastination?

How can you differentiate between productive rest and procrastination?

What does it mean to "shift your identity" when addressing procrastination?

Why is tracking your progress critical in developing new habits?

How does understanding the science of procrastination help you overcome it?

What is the link between emotional regulation and procrastination?

How can aligning tasks with your peak energy levels boost productivity?

Why should you focus on tasks that align with your core values?

What role does gratitude play in maintaining a productive mindset?

How can identifying your "why" help you stay motivated to take action?

What is the most important takeaway from *Procrastination Unlocked: The Science Behind*

16

NOTES